Take Me With You When You Go

For Patrick

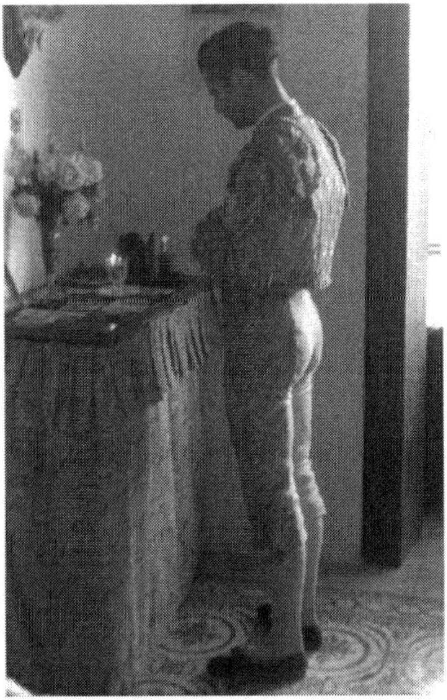

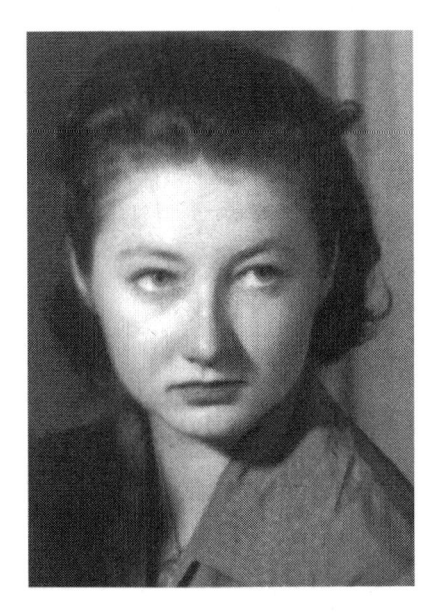

Stephanie at sixteen

I thank the following friends and readers who encouraged me to publish my Spanish memoir:
Patrick Early, Gisela Langsdorf, Bob and Jacky Linney, James Hogan, Jean Williams, Dermot Murphy, Hannah Wray, Matt Early, Shirley Hughes, Jim Slattery and Ronja Nylander Early.

Special thanks to:
Nigel Walkington for invaluable information, to Alyson Rose for editing and James Atkins for the book cover and so much more.

Antonio de Casas explained the mysteries of Semana Santa in Seville.

The verse on page 45 is from *Romance Sonámbulo,* first published in *Romancero Gitano* (1928) by Federico García Lorca.
The nursery ryhme on page 46 is from *Cuentos Infantiles* (1924) by Federico García Lorca.

All letters, verses, traditional lullabies and rhymes are translated by the author.

Preface

When clearing out drawers preparatory to moving house, I found a bundle of letters. The notepaper was parchment-like and bore a slight whiff of age. I recognised Javier's spidery writing — he who had befriended me in Jerez.

This was a souvenir of the time when Dublin was no place to be for a girl of sixteen without school examinations or family connections, and my Dominican school had arranged for me to be transported to Jerez de la Frontera, to live as an English-speaking "Miss" in a feudal Catholic family of great wealth and privilege.

The four girls whose lives I was expected to share were my contemporaries: thirteen and descending in age in steps of one year. They were children of the sherry aristocracy that had survived the brutal Spanish civil war of 1936 - 39 intact, returning from exile abroad to reclaim their estates when the coast was clear.

The family house was a lock-up. Elaborate security precautions meant that all comers had to pass through the single-entry guarded *portón* to gain admission to the family quarters and service areas.

Within the walls of the *palacio* obedience was total, there was never a hint of complaint or revolt from any member of the three-generation family, nor from the servants ranked hierarchically within.

Routine and order prevailed. Each person played a part in a rigid patriarchal system and the women of the house existed in self sacrificing sorority. As the days of my stay unravelled the role of dissenter, largely through inexperience, would fall to me.

The one-sided love affair revealed in the rediscovered letters became the basis for this Spanish memoir. It seems that despite the age difference between us, I had become quite involved with Javier – a torero who had not made the grade. I was caught up in his dreams, aspirations and disappointments although I knew nothing about him really. He was always respectful. His letters display candour and a clear voice across the decades. He worries about my health and wellbeing. Perhaps he was even sincere in his declarations of love and certainly in his desire for escape from the stultifying order imposed by the Franco apparatus, which reached into the very interstices of society. What we had in common was a feeling of entrapment, but in very different ways.

Whenever I thought about that interlude of my life, which ended abruptly and seemed like a calamity at the time, it was with optimism. After all Franco was not going to live for ever.

I had been out of my depth and had got into scrapes in

Jerez but despite the upsetting circumstances of my departure, I was much enriched by the experience. The only sad thing was the rupture with the girls. I never heard from them again. There was one final forlorn letter from Javier after my return home.

Chapter One

'It will be wonderful,' Ma said, 'an experience not to be foregone. You will meet all the best people in Spain.'

She had put my name forward for the position of "Miss" – a system designed for Irish Catholic girls to be billeted in aristocratic Spanish families so as to teach Spanish children English and share in their cloistered lives. Several girls would be going to Seville from my school.

'So you won't be on your own,' said Ma.

But I was the only candidate for a position in Jerez de la Frontera and she didn't bother to enquire whether Seville was nearby. No point in telling her I didn't want to go. Ma was adamant. I accepted that I had to leave Dublin, even though the thought of leaving my friends behind to start a new life elsewhere was unthinkable. I had no exam prospects, having failed to acquire the Irish language to a sufficient level at school. There didn't seem to be any clear way forward. I had no idea what I could do next. I would soon be sixteen and a solution had to be found.

I was also fed up with being alone at home with Ma, just

the two of us circling around each other day in and day out. There was no conflict between us we rubbed along. Ma didn't compete with me like some mothers did with their daughters. Neither did she provide moral support or guidance. She had given up on living when she became a widow and after her older children had left home. She imagined she was doomed, expecting imminently to follow her husband into the next world. In the meantime she lived a passive existence waiting for the day to come, content to sit bolt upright in her winged arm chair with the Irish Times and a packet of cigs on the armrest, swathed in silk scarves: she gloried in their colours – apricot, aquamarine and pink swirls on greys – as she did in the texture of her cashmere sweaters.

'I have had my life' she would tell me. 'It's your turn now. Make the most of it.' And I was left trying to work out how to live that life. Any demand I made on her was too much effort: preparing small meals, washing a few clothes in the sink and doing a little housework. It had all come to a head, I thought. I have become annoying to her and she wants me gone. So I would go. It was a gamble. Maybe going to Spain would work out well. Who was to know? Maybe I would meet new people and make a new life there.

So my protest was only half-hearted when the Spanish adventure presented itself.

'How would you like to be uprooted and sent away to God-knows-where?' I said. 'What if the people don't like me? Or, more to the point, what if I don't like them?'

'Of course they'll like you and I'm sure they'll be lovely people. It'll be just like being at home. After all, they are all Catholic, only they'll be speaking Spanish, which you'll be able to learn. Anyway what else are you going to do, a fatherless child like you and no examinations to your name?'

For her, this was the answer. In a single action my mother would be rid of me, shift the burden of her late adolescent child and at the same time some cachet would rub off and transform me in my absence. A finishing school gloss would envelop me. That's what she wanted. I would return a well-turned-out señorita.

'After all, it will only be for two years,' said Ma.

TWO YEARS! Who would remember me after two years? By then I would have disappeared from the lives of my friends and certainly from the face of County Dublin.

* * *

Preparations for me to leave Dublin went ahead. I was under age and would be travelling alone. The headmistress at my convent and the parish priest signed papers for me to be issued with the bottle-green passport of the Republic, a simple harp placed centrally on the cover. I would soon be on my way with a stopover in London, where my brother Paul would ferry me across the city from train to plane.

Ma raised enough energy to help me prepare and together with my married sister Rose we went shopping. We discussed what I would wear in Spain: whether to buy all cotton clothes for hot weather, especially as I was going to the south where it was always sunny, or whether I would need a coat, or a rain coat. Rose was of the opinion that it never rained in the south of Spain. We decided on a simple wardrobe of plain blouses and serge skirts. Ma selected a blue wool two-piece costume – my first costume. I wasn't sure if these clothes would be suitable for my new life. Neither was I sure about the pink pigskin court shoes she chose for me to wear with the suit.

The waiting period dragged on. Really, I just wanted to fade into the background of my life again, or else slip away quietly. I hated leaving Rose's children behind. At three and two years old, they probably would not even remember me after two years away. I feared they would transfer their affection to others – a thought hard to bear. My friends were envious that I was the one going away, taking a chance on another way of life. Those girls that spoke the Irish language would stay on to take the final certificate school exams. They had a future and a settled existence before them, but I would have to leave bound – like many others – for England and beyond.

For so many years, meeting the Dun Laoghaire Mailboat that crossed the Irish Sea to Wales had been part of my life – there was always someone coming or going. Now I was the one leaving. My friends came to see me off. I watched from the deck of the boat as their bicycles free-wheeled carelessly in circles around the bollards of Dun Laoghaire pier. They waved and shouted last messages from cupped hands as the ship left the harbour. Messages that I couldn't hear, because of the seagulls clamouring in excitement and the blast of the Mailboat foghorn.

***

A storm with lightning coincided with my first flight. The chair into which I was strapped held me in a close embrace while the ancient Spanish Iberia plane reared and bucked. The palms of my hands oozed cold sweat and my body was corpse-stiff with fear. Hours of waiting to fall out of the sky – the sheer terror of it!

When the plane touched down in Seville airport late at night, I was surprised to be alive. It was a hot night and I sweltered in my blue wool suit, the one Ma had bought for me at Brown Thomas's, the one she had deemed suitable to launch me into Spanish high society. Wrong. Wrong. Everything wrong. I knew my pink pigskin shoes with the low Cuban heels were ridiculous. But what did it matter? I could not prevail over circumstances. I would probably die soon anyway.

A man approached and made himself known. He guided me to a jeep-like car. Already I saw that all the elements of existence had been transformed. Instead of the soft greyness of my native suburb, with small plants arranged in front gardens and the sea always lapping in my ears – everything that I was used to – I saw waving palm trees. I saw red sky. I smelt sweet perfume on the air and strange tobacco and dust. I heard different pitched voices from those I knew, shouting and laughing.

The driver drove me along a sand-coloured highway into a sand-coloured city of softly lit narrow streets. Arriving at a red brick building on a corner, he manoeuvred through iron gates into a courtyard, where several shiny cars were parked very closely together between built-up beds of large-leafed vegetation.

A thin woman dressed in black came to meet me from the glass doorway of the Seville house I would come to know as the Palacio Solís in the Calle Sierpes. She spoke an exact, hesitant English.

'Welcome,' she said. 'You will stay here tonight with me and tomorrow you will go to Jerez de la Frontera and there you will meet the girls. They are not much younger than you. My granddaughters Blanca and Fatima will be your charges, and Maria Antonia and Mariana too, and maybe even Mercedita – but she is only four and too young to learn English. But you are tired,' said the woman. 'You will rest now.'

I was grateful for the kindness in her demeanour but too overcome with fatigue and shyness to converse. I was uncomfortable in my blue wool suit. My pink shoes pinched.

'I will send a tray to your room. What would you like to eat?'

'Just a glass of milk, please,' I said, longing for the comfort of something familiar.

'Milk,' she said. 'And fruit, and biscuits perhaps. Sleep well now, child. They will take you to your room.'

I followed the uniformed maid who took my bags along wood-panelled corridors to a wood-panelled room where a tray of food had been prepared. The door closed and I confronted the first of many meals I would eat on my own in my room during my time in Spain. I fell on the glass of milk.

But it was not the milk I knew. It was disgusting. Strong-tasting, grey liquid with bits of skin floating on the surface clogged up my mouth and assaulted my senses. Now I would really die, I thought, gagging, without my fresh, white Irish milk.

Chapter 2

The following day, after my first drive through the plains of Andalusia, I came to the tall terraced house on a *plaza* in Jerez de la Frontera. It had an imposing façade and a large covered entrance with a great wrought iron gate. Another woman of Spain dressed in black came out on to the pavement to welcome me. She was Dolores, the servant of the children's mother. She took me in a small lift to the second floor, where four little girls dressed in matching gingham dresses sat at a dining table in a wide corridor. They didn't leave the table or crowd around when I arrived – any excitement they felt at meeting a new companion who spoke English was kept firmly under control.

'I am Blanca,' said the eldest girl in English. She had obviously been practising for this moment and took responsibility for her sisters and the introductions. 'Welcome to Jerez.'

Soft footsteps preceded the arrival of their mother, Doña Mariana. Slim and quietly spoken; she seemed very unassuming for the mistress of such a grand house. She had a brilliant warm smile and I was immediately attracted to her. She bade the girls show me around and told them that, above all, they had to speak only English to me on every occasion. She explained that the children had never had a "Miss" before, and any English they knew was from school.

So I became the English-speaking companion to four little Spanish girls: Blanca, twelve; Fatima, eleven; Maria, nine and Mariana, eight years old. They lived, and now I would too, in a feudal household on the edge of the town of Jerez de la Frontera. The family bodega of San Patricio sherry was around the corner.

I became acquainted with all those dwelling within the house: the children, the parents of the children, the grandparents, the servants and those who acted as intermediaries between the almost-enclosed household and the outside world. I was subject to the very strict rules prevailing for girls, which I was bound to accept – at least I would have to try and accept them. Really life in Dublin had been free by comparison. Being a "Miss" was not a real job at all. It meant hanging around all day waiting for something to happen. It was especially hard during those first days of that summer term while I struggled to accept the limitations and restrictions placed on my life.

There was too much time to contemplate my situation, time to brood and endless hours to kill. An average day involved an early breakfast with the girls before they went to school, and then a long gap until they came home again for lunch at three in the afternoon.

Apart from keeping them company when they were at

home and being one of their number (although I was not really one of them) my only occupation was to learn the language of the people amongst whom I found myself. This I did quite unselfconsciously, without resort to study.

At first I picked up greetings: *hola, buenos días, buenas noches, adios*: and then phrases and exclamations; simple words to make myself acceptable: *¡Qué bien! me gusta, vale,* and suchlike comments. In a short time I could string a sentence together, memorising the words to be used in the right order and in the right situation and I carefully copied intonation and pronunciation. I practised hard until I could get my tongue around the unfamiliar new sounds.

I was mostly restricted to the quarters of the older *niñas*. When they came home from school, Pepa, our designated maid, served lunch – *almuerzo* – on the vast table in the wide corridor outside our bedrooms. I heard her draw near, carrying trays of food deftly aloft on her shoulder, along the corridors and down the stairs from the kitchen on the top floor to this dining room in a corridor which was also our living room. Between meals and whenever there was free time after the girls had done their homework, we played cards or quiet board games at the all-purpose table. Austerity was the mood of the house: simple ways and a disciplined routine. We didn't have a playroom or other inviting unsupervised space, a place where we could dress up, play boisterously or giggle helplessly as girls like to do.

Neither was my room a place of relaxation. It was sparsely furnished with a high single bed and built-in wardrobe. A small table and chair in one corner served as a desk and allowed me to read and write without sitting on the bed. At times during the day I would get onto the bed but jumped up when anyone was around, so no visitor would find me lolling about. I made sure I was always seen to be at my desk; fully dressed and patiently reading the books sent from home. I did not want to give an impression of idleness or be found daydreaming. I never lowered my guard.

There must be life outside in the *plaza*, I imagined, beyond the metal-framed door and the window with heavy wooden shutters, which took up the external wall of the room and gave on to a terrace. The shutters were lowered at night so as to create a place of total darkness and prevent one from waking too early in the morning; or lowered during siesta to exclude the light of day, allowing no chink to pass through. Sometimes I stepped out on to the terrace during the day to see what was going on in the plaza. But there was never anything going on, I was mistaken in thinking that there was. It was too hot to be outside and the blinding sun, which cast long contrasting shadows, hurt my eyes.

I looked for ways to amuse myself. I even wondered if I could adopt a small pet for company. That could not be, I was informed, as animals only lived in the country. There were no pets – and certainly no dogs – in town houses. Where would they go? There were only internal patios, or else enclosed gardens like that of the Bodega Garvey, where I had noticed a few families of skinny cats.

My employers were the owners of this garden, set in the centre of the bodega, where the dry sherry known as San Patricio was matured and stored. It was said that this fine dry sherry was unique amongst all the sherries of Jerez de la Frontera and held its own with those of more famous bodegas: Domecq, Gonzalez Byass, Sandeman or Osborne.

At weekends we went to the *casa de campo* with Jesus, our driver, in the car of the older girls. The smaller children also came: four-year-old Mercedita; Javier, the first son of the Morenes family, three, and Paco, two years old. They came with their driver and their nurse, Tata. She went by no other name. This was the only place where all the brothers and sisters played together. But really the *casa de campo*, in the countryside some way out of Jerez, was very disappointing – just a small pavilion on a patch of crab grass, too tough to sit on and plagued with *rosetta,* a nasty grass thistle, and beset with biting ants.

Tata was not young and very overweight. She wore her long hair in a stringy bun. She keeled to one side, as she sidled like a crab along the corridors of the second floor of the Palacio Garvey, hugging the wall while toting a baby on her best hip. Although fresh every day, her uniform was always grubby from the various excretions of the *niños menores* – those substances which formed my first Spanish vocabulary: *moco, kaka, pipi, vómitos.*

From Tata, I also learned my first Spanish nursery rhymes in the boredom of those afternoons in the *casa de campo*. She sang nonsense songs to the children, rhyming words in sequences, with no particular meaning, in clear staccato rhythms and in the gravel, flamenco voice of Andalusia:

A-zer-ín, A-zer-ón, Las Cam-pa-nas de San Juan.

From her, I learned about the mythical Spanish bogey

man – the *coco* that comes to snatch naughty children and with which Tata threatened her charges if they didn't drop off to sleep immediately at siesta time – here comes the bogey man. And he takes away the children, that don't go to sleep, *que viene el co-co, y se llev-a a los ni-ños, que duer-men po-co.* That is, when she wasn't comforting them and calling each one her sunshine, pressing them to her vast breast – *A ro- ro mi ni-*ño*, a ro-ro mi sol.*

* * *

Once, Señorita – an additional companion for the girls without the prestige of the English language at her disposal – escorted us to the cinema. Señorita, who, like Tata, went by no other name – was of indeterminate middle age and dumpy because she was sedentary. She habitually wore fashionable tartan and usually carried needlework in a tapestry bag. Her dentistry was elaborate and the metal in her mouth made speech difficult for her. She was really our chaperone, a role which gave her permission to be an adept informant, a proficient tell-tale tit. She always reported our activities to the senior members of the household. As we were all girls, she was especially keen to see we didn't mix or have contact with any member of the opposite sex, in the garden, at the cinema or anywhere else we might go.

The Cine Jerezano showed Walt Disney films and Fred Astaire romances: *Grandes títulos de estreno* – Best and newest Releases, proclaimed from its posters. The most exciting film of the season was the German musical, *La Familia Trapp*, telling the story of a young novice, Maria, sent by her convent to care for the children of the Baron Von Trapp upon the death of his wife. She makes a great success of her time with the seven children, teaching them songs and eventually creating a famous choir. Against her wishes, the Reverend Mother persuades her to marry the Count, even though she is still a nun, so she can become a permanent fixture in the family and a proper mother to the children. Maria also manages to save the family from the Nazi soldiers that occupy Austria. I identified with Maria Von Trapp. There were obvious parallels with my own life, even though I wasn't a nun and unlikely to ever become one. I imagined myself in her position although I hoped never to have to shoulder great responsibility as she did. If war ever came to Jerez de la Frontera I would be stuck with the children as she was. I would have to smuggle them home to Ireland! (I did not realise then that bitter war had already taken place in the town where I was living. I would learn about that later).

The cinema was full of young adolescent girls the same age as we were. The air was static with our yearnings. On one occasion we saw the musical South Pacific, a short version because General Franco, who ruled Spain, made sure we didn't see anything inappropriate. He ordered unsuitable bits of American films to be cut. They were also dubbed into a strange clipped version of Spanish, making it difficult for a foreign person to understand what was happening.

It was at the Cine Jerezano that I was initiated into the delights of eating sunflower seeds – *pipas* – while gazing at the screen. These came in a screw of newspaper made into a cornet container. I learned to crack the seed by placing the shell width-wise between the teeth, biting to release the contents for a slight musty taste to invade the taste buds. There was no substance to the seed, just the pleasure of the tiny sound when the case burst. We *niñas* sighed in satisfaction when the film came to an end, replacing handkerchiefs – damp from tears of excitement shed – to pockets and stepping over the mound of sunflower seed husks spilling out from under each wooden seat.

Although I did not seriously imagine that my fate would be linked with the Spanish family in such a way that I would end up married to my employer like Maria von Trapp, I did hope romance of some kind would come my way during my two-year exile. I knew I caused a stir in the *bodega* garden.

The boys that worked in the bodega heaved and shifted oak-wood barrels of *San Patricio* sherry from one level to another. They turned and rolled the barrels over to stir up the contents and allow air to circulate at the correct temperature around the maturing wine: they whistled and sang songs as they worked. They were interested in *my* movements and curious about the pale, blond foreign girl that I was – a stranger amongst them.

I noticed that instead of entering the vaulted cavern of the bodega through the front entrance, they would use the side door with access from the built-up garden, where we *niñas* sat with jasmine growing around our bower and where aspidistras flourished in large terracotta pots. Sometimes a boy would smile and wink at me over the beds of vivid, red geraniums, which separated us. They would never dare speak. But before long their interest in my presence had been noted and reported to Doña Mariana by Señorita. After that we had to go to the *casa de campo* more often than ever and we only rarely went to the bodega garden for fear that the boys there would intrude on our isolation.

* * *

'You must register with the police,' said Doña Mariana, several weeks after my arrival when she paid a visit to my room on the second floor.

Given the lack of excitement so far, the idea of a visit to the police station for my passport to be stamped looked like being an adventure. I thought I would get to know Jerez, and one day I would be able to find my way around by myself. Apart from the cinema visit, I hadn't left the immediate neighbourhood yet. Being an independent girl, I knew every one of my home streets in the suburbs of Dublin. It didn't occur to me that similar exploration would not be possible in Jerez.

A time was arranged for Señorita to accompany me one evening after siesta. Together we walked sedately along the narrow streets from the Plaza Arenal to the Cuartel San Agustin for the first of my three-monthly visits to the office of the Guardia Municipal in an imposing building with "*Todo por la Patria*" emblazoned over the *portón*.

After a considerable wait in an antechamber I was invited to enter an office, which smelt overwhelmingly of tobacco. I presented my green passport for inspection to the Guardia, who sat under a portrait of General Franco.

The Guardia smoked small cigars of the blackest tobacco. From where he sat he directed phlegm deftly into a nearby metal-rimmed bowl – a spittoon – on the floor which contained enough water to allow small islands of yellow phlegm to float in their own sea. There was much commentary, which on subsequent occasions I came to understand, about what foreigners – *extranjeras* – thought they were doing in Spain making a nuisance of themselves. He stamped my passport with a rubber seal moistened in a pad of red ink and terminated the business by getting to his feet and standing ramrod straight (for this was 1958) to say: "*Arriba España*" and "*Viva Franco*" the signal for Señorita and myself to leave the room and the building and make our way back down the Calle Jose Antonio, to the Palacio Garvey.

* * *

The visit to the police station was an intimidating experience, but the walk back through the streets was an ordeal of magnitude, with or without the company of a Señorita. I didn't understand why I was being repeatedly accosted: a boy or a man would alter his stride to keep pace, stick his face close to mine and sigh painfully. Apart from the phrase "*madre mía*", I was in the dark as to what was being said. Why would a man fall into step to thrust his face into mine and speak with great intensity? This was a fearful intrusion. No wonder I could never be allowed out alone. Señorita did not enlighten me as to why the men did this. She was severe and unapproachable. She ignored all such attentions and pushed me along, never glancing to right or left, only stopping occasionally to talk to someone she knew. She breathed a sigh of relief when she got me back to the house.

I knew I annoyed her in some way, but didn't know why. In fact I couldn't make any headway with Señorita. Not because of the language barrier but more because we had nothing whatsoever to say to each other. We shared little common ground, coming, as we did, from different countries, speaking different languages and having no shared values apart from Catholic ones, which translated differently in different places. I was used to too much freedom growing up in County Dublin with only my benevolent mother to reign me in, while Senorita was used to being locked indoors, mistrusting all advances from humankind and avoiding as far as possible the harassment of the streets.

Chapter Three

The Palacio Garvey took up one side of the Plaza del Arenal. In the centre of the square, seated on a monument in the middle of a fountain, a statue of Miguel Primo de Rivera, the former prime minister of Spain, rose up against the sky.

At half-past nine every night, the wrought-iron gate of our *palacio* – that *portón* of intimidating dimensions – was closed with a clang by José the porter.

As the time drew near, I watched from the covered terrace outside my room as the maids of the household, including Pepa, left their *novios* – each dressed in the uniform of their military service – in the long shadows of Primo de Rivera's fountain. They scurried across the plaza to reach the house before it shut down.

I wondered what the rush was about and what the consequences would be of being locked out. Why was the time so fixed? Were we locked up to keep the girls in, or the boys out? Both, I thought, as men and women lived separate lives. The men went away as every single young man in Spain had to do the *mili,* said Pepa. They went to a barracks, which could be anywhere in the country, for two years military service. Two years! That was the same period of time I would be spending in Spain. Thenceforth I would think of this time as my own personal *mili*.

I would be part of the household and find my place, because everyone knew their place in Spain. Even the children were all dressed exactly the same: same frocks, same shoes, same socks. The servants – both men and women – all wore uniforms to denote status and rank. There was even something military about José the porter, guarding the house in a double-breasted navy uniform, which made even the most unprepossessing of men, as he was, look important. He behaved like a policeman and, despite being married to Carmen the cook, spent the night as well as the day in his porter's room, making sure that anyone entering or leaving the building came under his scrutiny.

After the great houses of Jerez de la Frontera closed down for the night, the *Sereno* would appear on the streets. I saw him pass by when I stepped out onto the balcony into the night air heavily scented with orange blossom. He was the night watchman who walked the streets of Jerez until daybreak, keeping the inhabitants safe. Attached to his leather belt, he carried a heavy set of iron keys – the keys of the houses he was patrolling. Those who had been out late – and people stayed out very late – summoned him by clapping their hands sharply and then he came running to open their doors.

The children told me that Generalísimo Franco wanted the people of Spain to be safe in their beds and that was the *Sereno*'s job. He would notice if any stranger was abroad at night and if he blew his whistle piercingly, the *Guardia* would come to investigate.

In Ireland, I told them, we didn't need anyone to keep us safe at night as people went to bed early and the streets *were* safe, so we had no such person. It was a very old profession, they said, and they taught me the song the *Sereno* used to sing in ancient times as he passed by, hour upon hour, declaring the serenity of the streets: two o'clock, three o'clock, four o'clock have chimed and all serene: *las dos, las tres, las cuatro han dado y sereno.* The other sound of the night, as well as the hand claps summoning the *Sereno*, was the tolling of the church bells from Santo Domingo or the church of San Miguel, heard from the other side of town once the traffic had subsided.

* * *

The grandparents, the old Marqueses, occupied the bottom floor of the Jerez house. The parents of the children, Francisco de Morenés, son of the Marqués, and Mariana Solís, from a well-known Seville family, lived on the first floor. The chapel, where the household heard mass, was also on the first floor. Several times a week a priest would cross the plaza from the ancient church of Santo Domingo bearing the beige satin-covered, silver ciborium containing the Blessed Sacrament. He would sweep through the *portón* to enter the little wrought-iron lift, which carried him to the chapel, boxed up in all his vestments.

As a special privilege we, the *niñas mayores,* were allowed to attend mass in the chapel at weekends. We crowded into the small windowless room hung with satin tapestries. The marble altar had a gold painted lamb-of-god at the centre. There was a virgin and child to one side and the Archangel Michael on the other.

The old Señores sat on two well-padded chairs with matching kneelers. We sat on benches against the back wall. The small space was stuffy, especially when the priest swung the incense burner of perfumed fumes. Because of the confined space and the solemnity of the occasion I would be stricken with an attack of suppressed laughter. The girls took everything so seriously. If they noticed me coughing attempting to control the paroxysms, they pretended not to notice. They resisted contagion, never succumbed to the urge.

We shared our confined quarters on the second floor with Tata and the toddlers. Our most constant visitor there was Doña Mariana. But she was pregnant with her eighth child and didn't always feel well, so there were many days when she didn't appear at all.

When her husband, Don Francisco, came to kiss the girls good night, he would often drop in to see me in the adjoining bedroom. He would sit on my bed for a chat in English and stay quite some time to tell me about the day's hunting in the *campo,* or of his trip to Madrid, where he belonged to a smart set which included the film star Ava Gardner. I wasn't put out by his visits. There was nothing personal in his conversation. I imagined he spoke in the same way to anyone who would listen. The household didn't provide many opportunities for him to speak English, the language of his school days. I thought he looked exactly like his baby son: his big bald head, enormous blue eyes and candid smile.

If both parents were too busy then Dolores came to see us. Dolores was the *doncella de confianza* – Doña Mariana's trusted ladies' maid. A stately woman of authority, her black uniform and starched white apron signified her rank. She never wore the ordinary gingham of the lesser maids who did the cleaning. She never raised her voice beyond a murmur. On rare occasions when I visited the first floor I would sometimes meet her in the corridors carrying armfuls of snow-white, lace-edged linen or else carrying a tray of camomile tea, served in a delicate china cup and saucer, to her mistress, now confined to bed with a difficult pregnancy.

Our maid, Pepa, was a rough girl by comparison. Pepa chided us all. She swore and blustered in common Andaluz, chivvying the girls to hurry up, to stand up straight, not to be silly, to take their clothes off the bed: *anda ya niña, date prisa. Anda ya. Rápido…*

My companions, when they weren't at school where I should have been, were the two elder girls: Blanca, who was a swot, with large dark eyes and two little pigtails. She was always interested in the natural phenomena we encountered in the countryside. Or she would provide the historical explanations for life in Jerez or Sevilla. She had an explanation for why Jerez was sometimes known as Xerez with an X – with pronunciation called a jota in Spanish – like a "Ka" in English, from the times when Moors from Morocco lived in Jerez. It was from the Arabic way of saying it, although sometimes it was called "*Seres*" without a hard letter.

Fatima had short hair and a good sense of humour. She told jokes and made us laugh. She knew all the verses and rhymes. The next girl down in age, Maria Antonia, sometimes tagged along; she was over-shadowed by her sisters. The fourth girl, Marianita, was delightful and accomplished. She could sing, dance and act better than the others and brought gaiety wherever she went. These sisters were peas in a pod, tightly bonded and implicitly understanding each other. Although I shared their lives I knew I was never to become a part of their family. Anyway, apart from all their cousins, they had no need of others to widen their tight circle.

I came to resent the fact that my schooling had been curtailed. Even though I had disliked the boredom of the classroom and had escaped whenever I had the opportunity, I now decided that school was definitely more exciting than being stuck in the Palacio Garvey. At home in Dublin I had known great freedom; I was free to meander abroad on my bicycle, free to go to a tennis club dance with Josie, who always smelt of biscuits. She was the friend Ma disapproved of because she came from a large family and lived in corporation housing in Sallynoggin. I also had my friend Michael, a boy who used to come looking for me. Together we escaped from the groups congregating at the school gates in the long afternoons. And I had my married sister with two children who loved me. In Jerez, I was locked up and friendless.

I tried my best to teach the girls English, but actually my Spanish progressed at a much faster rate because of the need for communication and – apart from contact with the children's parents – the lack of anyone with whom to speak my own language. Soon I learned to prattle with the girls and also with the servants upstairs on the *azotea,* the area on the flat-roof from where you could see all the other flat roofs of the city, with their laundries and clothes-lines all at different levels, stretching far into the distance. This *azotea* was the service area for the running of the *palacio*, where cooking, washing and ironing all took place. A world apart, it was also the living quarters of the servants and I was driven up there in search of company during the long tedious days. Here were the stone sinks for soaking, bleaching, beating, and starching, as well as huge mangles for wringing the clothes.

Several women came from town to do the laundry. They sang songs as they squeezed, rubbed and pummelled. They hung the washing out, two of them carrying the large sheets, which they stretched and shook with a cracking sound to hang on the many lengths of clothes-lines to drip and dry for a matter of hours in the intense heat of the roof terrace. Other women did expert ironing, folding and pressing, reducing the size of sheets and clothing to take up the least space.

Señorita Marta, an impoverished gentlewoman, came to do the mending on an ancient Singer sewing machine; a pile of linen awaited her attention every week. She also neatly darned any holes she found in clothing and worked through a great pile of socks. She was hungry, I thought, as she lunched with us on the second floor and not with the servants upstairs. This was her square meal of the week. She squirreled away titbits in a serviette to take home to her mother and sister. Life was hard on women living alone in Jerez and Señorita Marta was a breadwinner. The laundry women had lunch at Carmen's big table at 2 pm and left before *siesta*. I envied those who came and went to the Palacio Garvey – even Señorita Marta. At least they all had some independence. They were of a superior species to those of us locked up in the house with no possibility of communication with the outside world. Those of us who lived with the children were incommunicado, as were the personal maids responsible for each group: the old *señores marqueses,* the *señores, niñas mayores* and *niños menores.* The assistant cook and two scullery maids lived in small, undecorated rooms and spent all their time in the kitchen. Sometimes I too would spend time at the large table in the kitchen with the servants, just for the company.

Carmen, the cook, seldom left her position in the rooftop kitchen, even though her husband, José the porter, lived in his cubbyhole beside the *portón.* In fact, each person was almost always in his or her habitual place, given that half-days off only occurred on a fortnightly basis. It was always a shock to see Carmen in normal clothes on the rare occasions she went out carrying a smart handbag and looking like a proper Señora in high-heeled shoes and stockings with a straight seam up the back instead of rope-soled *alpargatas.*

No one worked as hard as Carmen. She prepared endless cycles of food, from paps and purees for the babies and toddlers to a light diet for the elders and wonderful fine cooking for those in between. She also catered for the servants, who could help themselves from pots of stews made from lentils and chickpeas.

Sometimes I would help Pura – short for Purificación – an old retainer, who had once been the *doncella* to the

Marquesa. She too never left the roof-top kitchen. Any family she must once have had had long since evaporated. Together we would shell great mounds of fresh peas, or top and tail green beans, or peel a sack of potatoes. Sometimes the women would engage in bawdy chat. Perhaps because we were confined, street-wise cracks often took over in the *azotea*, where I gleaned some very sketchy ideas about the mysteries of life in Andalusia. Certainly the talk was of an earthier nature than any discussion on a similar subject in Ireland, where I had been kept in ignorance and innocence, and where only an occasional lapse in the guard of adults gave me a clue as to the facts of life into which I had yet to be initiated. In the Spanish kitchen the younger women gave vent, comparing with graphic gestures the attributes of their *novios*. They lived in a community of women, because the *mili* had disrupted their lives by taking the men away. Pepa was the exception. The young man paying court to her had already completed the *mili*. She gave us the full rundown on her love life in pantomime. We would laugh helplessly, crying with mirth. I learnt that the word for cackles was *carcajadas*. I also learned many other words that I had never known before in any language and could not imagine ever using.

Pura asked Pepa if she had permission to be with the boy she was seeing. Had she told Dolores about him? Was he a suitable *novio*? Maybe he was a *rojo*, in which case she would have to work forever, as no *rojo* would ever get a job in Franco's Spain. He would have to hide underground like a mole – *un topo*.

'*Cállate le boca, vieja. Tú que sabes.*' said Pepa dangerously, telling the old lady to shut her mouth. She easily lost her temper. She could keep up a stream of abuse until her opponents fell silent.

Dolores hardly ever came to the kitchen. She was too busy with her linen to engage in banter. All gossip would stop when she entered the room in deference to her seniority.

Sometimes we sang songs, one of which was about Primo de Rivera, the "*señorito de Jerez*" sitting on his horse with one raised hoof outside in the plaza. They would tell me how he would ride off with the gypsies roistering – *de juerga* – leaving all responsibilities behind. How he had become the Prime Minister of Spain and was the father of José Antonio, founder of the *Falangist* movement – whatever that was – who had been martyred and killed by the *rojos,* whoever they were. The song said that in Jerez there was a plaza with a gold and silver fountain and there was a horse in the middle, on top of which sat Primo de Ribera.

Jer-ez de la Front-er-a tiene un-a plaza, tiene una plaza
Con un-a fuen-te al medio que es de or-o y pla-ta
de oro y plata
y un cab-al-lo y en-ci-ma
Primo Rib-er-a
Primo de Ribera

It was intolerably hot upstairs during siesta, while I waited for the girls to come home from school. Eventually the women fell silent and a torpor would descend upon us. As the heat intensified, the only sounds came from the cicadas outside that got noisier and noisier as well as the rip and crack of hand-held fans of pleated material, as they were closed and reopened at intervals.

Chapter Four

Sometimes my employers relaxed the strict regime for my supervision and allowed Pilar, the Señorita from the Domecq family, to take me for an outing. We went to the Hotel Los Cisnes, on the Calle Jose Antonio, which was the main meeting place for foreigners in Jerez. It was supposed that I would meet other English-speaking people there.

But I didn't meet any foreigners, only the idle sons (never daughters) of sherry families. Often these *señoritos*, scented lightly with *agua de colonia*, their fine heads greased with *gomina* – the Brylcream local men used to slick back their hair – had been educated at Catholic boarding schools in England. They wore a uniform of flannel trousers and navy blazers with shiny buttons. They were pleasant conversationalists and had good manners, rather like Francisco, when he came to my room for a bedtime chat, on those occasions when he was in Jerez and not in Madrid with Ava Gardner and his filmmaker friends.

They drank *copas* of dry sherry – the *finos* of their bodegas – and smoked little cheroots. Although by no means part of their set, Pilar had established herself as a regular and was accepted by them. I tagged along and accepted the sweet wines – the syrupy olorosos and Pedro Jimenez varieties of sherry – that they offered as a suitable ambrosia for someone of tender years. Pilar made sure I didn't become tipsy. The men sat on tall stools at the bar while we sat in comfortable low chairs at a finely polished, glass-topped table, which acted as a barrier between us and them.

It was at Los Cisnes that I met Javier, who wasn't from a sherry family. He said he had once been a bullfighter. He was a small man, neat of hands and feet. His hair was smooth and sticky from *gomina* and he had a warm, sweet smile and a light voice – a bit like a girl really. A bullfighter needed to be small, nifty and neat, which he was. With me, he immediately adopted an easy intimacy.

'We will be friends,' he said. 'I will tell you all about Andalusia and you will get to know us well. You will get to know me well also.' He laughed when I tried out my Spanish. '*¿Pero qué dices?*' he said. 'What are you talking about?' He didn't understand a word of English, not a word.

His teeth were very white and small and, apart from the hint of a gold one next to one of his incisors, they matched the whiteness of his bleached shirt which he wore unbuttoned to reveal a V of hairless brown flesh. He wore black trousers and moccasin shoes with no socks. He was just about the same height as I was and he never kept still; quicksilver, he waltzed up to me when I appeared.

He was very anxious to work abroad, he said, and I could tell him how life was in other places. He said we could exchange letters so as to improve my Spanish. It would be good practice. I thought it would be hard work. I really only intended to be able to speak with people and understand what was going on. I never envisaged putting pen to paper. I thought it was odd to be writing to someone who lived in the same town and I couldn't imagine why somebody as old as Javier – the same age as Paul – would want to be friends with me.

He asked if we could meet up if ever I had a day off and could get away from the house alone. I said I would have to ask for permission to meet him and that I still wasn't sure I could find my way around. If we did meet it would have to be after the summer holidays. By that time I would be more confident.

'Never mind' he said, "I'll write to you in the meantime.'

Several days later I found a letter at the side of my plate: the spidery handwriting on parchment, which was to become so familiar, the envelope lined with purple tissue paper.

> *Querida Estefanía,*
>
> *This is the first of many letters I will write to you. You and I will find each other in writing. I am so glad to have met you and I want you to know that we will always be friends. You will see how rewarding it will be to have a Spanish friend.*
>
> *I want to tell you everything about myself. I have just eaten my supper – it was a very digestible rabbit stew and caused me no suffering at all. I had a small glass of wine to celebrate meeting you but generally I hardly drink at all. Bullfighters can't risk a drink. They must be absolutely sober at all times. Otherwise they could become disoriented in the bullring and miss their footing at a*

crucial moment and be gored. The bull would sense any distraction in a moment.

More out of boredom with my inactivity than a desire to communicate with Javier, I decided to respond. I chose my writing materials carefully at the nearby *Papelería*, a shop dedicated to the sale of all kinds of stationary: copybooks, pens, paper and ink – all lavish and extravagant. So much choice! I bought the same single sheets of parchment notepaper that Javier had used in writing to me. I bought violet ink to match the purple tissue paper lining the envelopes.

Back in my room I penned a few sentences with the aid of my small Collins Spanish Dictionary to check the spelling. I learned about the use of Spanish accents to add emphasis to syllables in words and how to put a squiggle over the "n" to make the sound for "*niñas*" – **ninyas.** Blanca answered any grammar or spelling questions that came up. I didn't tell her why I had become interested in writing, just in case writing letters to someone local was forbidden. I added a postscript in English saying I hoped he would understand my meaning. I directed the letter to Javier Gonzalez, in the Calle San Juan de Dios.

Carmen took me to the round-fronted Correos building, where I bought stamps – all with the portrait of General Franco's head, in different colours for the different denominations. Local blue stamps for writing to Javier and international red ones for the letters home to Ireland. I deposited my letters in the big yellow post box. It was a satisfying exercise.

A response from Javier came by return of post.

Querida Estefanía,

A few minutes ago I met the postman in the street who gave me a pile of business letters and amongst them was yours, which delighted me. I think that postmen are bringers of good and bad news. This was good so I invited him for a beer. I don't have to tell you that the first letter I opened was yours and I read it in seconds. I still haven't read the English part and I am impatient to know what it says…

Do you know something? We Spaniards are so careless in the way of affection that we don't care if we are being loved as long as we love. We are disinterested. We are above everything. However Spanish women want to be loved above all and then they love. That's curious, isn't it?

In love it is the one who loves the most who is happiest and I have a presentiment that I will grow to love you – or I am loving you – with all my heart.

* * *

Pepa served our meals on the all-purpose table in the wide corridor outside our bedrooms. She got us up in the morning with *café con leche* or *chocolate*, which we ate with sweet buns. I just drank water, unable to accept the cooked grey milk used to make the drinks, with grey *nata* floating on top. I never got used to it. The children came home from the convent for a copious late lunch at three o'clock. Then there was *merienda* at five o'clock: big chunks of salty bread with black chocolate. We had a light supper at nine before retiring to our rooms.

At first I hated the rigid routine of mealtimes and the

sheer quantities of food. But in time I developed a ravenous appetite. I anticipated meals, wondering what new taste would be presented to me. My great hunger drove me to be adventurous. I had thought of myself as a normal Irish girl, happy with a fry of bacon whenever I needed to eat, or sausages as a special treat, or else baked beans or cheese on toast.

But now I branched out. I discovered all the food of Spain, prepared expertly by Carmen and her team in the *azotea*. From *gazpacho andaluz* – the delicate salad soup of tomatoes, cucumbers, green peppers and bread, scented with old sherry vinegar from our bodega – to mounds of potato salad – *ensaladilla* – with a rich mayonnaise. I developed a passion for *milanesas* – bread-coated steaks – and chicken, *pollo en béchamel* and *croquetas* – also made with delicious white *béchamel*. I even ate *pajaritos* – small sparrow-like birds caught in a net. I think they were larks, and I stuffed them down, tearing off their tiny wings with my teeth as my tongue searched for another morsel of sweet flesh. I discovered the milk puddings of Spain: cream caramel, known as *flan,* and *crema catalana* and *arroz con leche*. I ate yoghurt laced with honey for the first time. Doña Mariana was very proud of a yoghurt maker she had bought on a visit to Paris. She carefully combined milk with a special powder bacillus, sticking her finger in the bowl to test if the milk was at blood temperature, before decanting the mixture into the little jars where fermentation took place.

Then, my exile's hunger still raging, I accompanied Señorita to the *Pastelería Moderna*, where together we scoffed string-like, glistening, eggy cakes, *cabello de angel* or angel's hair and *yemas* – the sweetened yolk of an egg. We ate delicate biscuits and crescent-shaped buns called half moons – *medias lunas*. We ate *palmitos* – pastries fashioned to look like palm leaves. Señorita said all the cakes were made by cloistered nuns – the Poor Clares; so we felt virtuous while indulging ourselves.

Soon I became as podgy as Señorita, who was now my ally – finally I had got through to her. I shared her sedentary way of life and her pursuit of consolation in sweetmeats. My thighs rubbed together unpleasantly when I walked in the heat. Instead of racing around the suburbs of Dublin on my bicycle, or going to tennis club hops where I burnt off surplus calories while teapot jiving to the emerging Nashville sounds of Chuck Berry and Elvis Presley with Josie from Sallynoggin, I now lusted for food.

At dead of night I crept up to the *azotea* to steal from the larder. So driven was I that I risked being discovered abroad in the large house when everyone else was asleep. I lost my fear of bumping into any ghost that might appear; those that lurked around corners, waiting to pull my hair or trip me up or make faces at me as I crept along the corridors that separated the different quarters. I ascended the staircase in bare feet feeling my way along the walls in the darkness. Arriving at the top I pushed through double swing door into the open area sometimes bathed in moonlight shining through the big windows. I crept past the kitchen dressers casting grey unfamiliar shadows before me, transforming the scene I knew so well by day. I found my way to the pantry where food was laid out under domed muslin covers.

I went in search of *chorizo* – a red spicy sausage – and white ham, and cured ham with cheese – *Jamón de York* and *Jamón Serrano con queso*. And *membrillo*, the wonderful quince paste eaten with cheese; and even olives, a taste for which it had taken me some time to acquire. I hadn't known any of these foods before and did not know, for example, that a quince was like a large, tough apple. There was such variety of food – whereas at home everything was plain. An apple was an apple and ham was ham and a sausage a sausage, there were no *types* of apples or ham or sausages.

I became fat, apathetic and lack-lustre. Doña Mariana commented on the change in my appearance when she came to visit the *niñas mayores*. What has happened to this girl who has become so fat?

'*La niña se ha puesto muy gorda,*' she said to Pepa. '*¿Qué le pasa?*'

I could have told her myself why I had become so fat: out of boredom, inactivity and homesickness. "I'll take her to see my doctor in Sevilla," she said.

Chapter Five

On the way to her mother's house in Sevilla (Seville had now become Sevilla to me as I became familiar with local names), Doña Mariana raised a sensitive topic.

'Your Spanish is good now' she said, 'but you must pay attention to forms of address. In Spanish there are different levels of respect and you can't just say "*tu*" to everybody. There are two ways of saying "you". 'It is quite all right for you to call the children "*tu*" but you must use "*usted*" as well. For example when you talk to me, you must say "*usted*". Also when you address my husband, Don Francisco, and other relatives, my sister Mati and the servants. You must call the senior servants Dolores and also Carmen the cook "*usted*". This will require much greater attention to detail.'

I was crushed by the criticism and embarrassed not to have picked this up for myself.

'But Blanca and Fatima say "*tu*" to everybody and to me,' I said.

'Yes, but they are children and they are speaking to members of their own family. Soon people will say "*usted*" to them and they will use "*usted*" to everybody too – except of course their parents,' she said, 'and their friends and you too of course, as you are almost the same age as they are. It's quite all right to say "*tu*" to your friends,' she said, smiling.

'But I don't have any friends,' I told her.

* * *

In the Palacio Solís on the Calle Sierpes in Sevilla, I was put to bed in a place smelling of honey from beeswax. It was hardly a room but one of a series of interconnecting state salons, with paintings on the walls. Facing me was a painting of the crucifixion. When meals were brought I could hear double doors opening and closing from far away – the sound muffled by shiny parquet floors and wood-panelled walls.

The doctor came to examine me with Doña Mariana and I heard them discuss my case. I was indeed "*muy gorda*". Despite all the eating, I was also anaemic and the doctor prescribed a horrible injection. I think it was intravenous iron. I lay in bed for a week looking at the painting on the wall: Christ hanging on the cross in a dark sky, his torso lengthened and his gaze directed upwards to a higher plane; the distant landscape was mountainous and in the foreground there was a tiny city in a hollow.

Doña Mariana came to visit every day after the painful injection. Sometimes her mother, the austere woman who had met me on my first night in Spain, came too. She carried her rosary in the pocket of her black dress and I could see her moving her fingers from one bead to the next, even while speaking, never stopping. She prayed constantly for the soul of her husband who had recently died, never forgetting him for a moment.

Doña Mariana told me that the painting on the wall was by Spain's great painter, El Greco, although he wasn't really Spanish, he was Greek, hence the name, and his paintings were very valuable. She said she would show me more Spanish paintings that I would probably like better, especially Murillo. She was sure I would prefer the Sevillian painter because he painted children and she knew I liked children. I would like the little boy eating grapes. Murillo painted girls as well and even the Virgin Mary was an ordinary girl for him. There were other Sevillian painters too, like Velasquez, but he had gone to the Spanish Court to paint the people there: the kings and queens and the Spanish princes and princesses, called *infantes* and *infantas*.

Taking pity on my solitude, she had found another Miss from Dublin to come and visit me. I wasn't too fond of Rita, the girl she found, whom I knew vaguely from my school. We had never got on. I was annoyed that she would see how fat I had become. I knew word would get back to Dublin telling of my pathetic state. I was also envious that she obviously had a much better social life in Sevilla, where there was a bigger circle of expatriates, while I was cut off in Jerez. However I cheered myself up when I realised that my Spanish was much better than hers. At least there was one advantage to my isolation. So I had to receive her with good grace and pretend I was having a good time. I was not having a good time, but

I hoped my social life would improve when I returned to Jerez

* * *

In the last weeks of her pregnancy Doña Mariana rarely came to the second floor. When she did appear she was drawn and tired. She stayed in her room until noon and moved with difficulty. Once she asked me to do up her shoes. I bent over her swollen legs and felt pity well up inside me. This is what Dolores feels, I thought as I pulled at the laces, pure pity for the suffering of this young woman, as she waited in a dark house with elderly parents for the birth of yet another child. The children were quite used to the absence of their mother. They didn't complain. They knew that the arrival of a new little brother or sister was imminent – a yearly event for them. Then she went to Sevilla.

Eventually she reappeared unencumbered and we were relieved that her ordeal was over. New baby Alfonso joined Tata, with Javier and Paco in the quarters of the *niños menores.* Mercedita – moved up with the big girls. At five years old, she was now with the *niñas mayores.*

Chapter Six

In Spain there is a saying: Don't take off your jacket until the fortieth of May! (*hasta cuarenta de Mayo, no se quita el sayo*); this caution because summer often doesn't come before June. Until then, we suffered from the cold inside the great, unheated house. The *azotea* was the only bright place. I was driven up there to the warmth of the sun, sitting outside with the flapping white sheets. I had grown tired of the antics in the kitchen and longed to be with people to whom I could relate easily. I longed to be in my own place with my own people where I would feel at ease. Homesickness gripped me. This was my punishment for not working harder. I had burnt my boats at school because I wasn't studious enough and didn't know enough Irish. If I was ever able to leave Jerez de la Frontera I would make sure that such a thing never happened to me again. Never again would I find myself in an unknown place without friends condemned to sit in the corridor of someone else's house.

Sometimes, on very chilly days, when the wind blew from the east, we were allowed into the grown-up sitting room to get warm. We sat at a round table covered in a heavy velvet cloth reaching to the ground. A brazier with live coals was placed inside the tent of it to keep our legs warm. The tablecloth never caught fire although the coals were bright and burning. We played *naipes* – a trick-taking card game, of four suits: coins, cups, sticks and swords (*oros, copas, bastos y espadas*).

When the cold easterly *levante* winds died out and warm air circulated again in the south, we emerged onto the streets after siesta for the evening *paseo*. Even we of the Palacio Garvey took to the plaza, where we walked about arm in arm with the rest of the population of Jerez. We dressed up to go out although we remained within sight of the *portón*. Tata put on a white uniform – dress and apron equally sparkling – and she dressed the toddlers, all smelling strongly of Agua de Colonia, in smocked outfits. Even the immaculate baby, habitually kept indoors, saw the evening light and the setting of the sun as his pram was proudly pushed up and down.

We bought sunflower seeds in a twist of newspaper from the man pushing his sweet-cart. We couldn't be seen eating them directly, but we would take them home for later. As dusk fell, groups of boys congregating around the fountain would start up *palmadas*, marking beats with their clapping: dull sounds from cupped hands or sharp sounds with three fingers finding the "hot" spots on their left hands. A photographer with a large camera on a tripod always occupied the same corner of the square. He disappeared under a black hood to take photos of passers-by and developed the film on the spot. He would snap individuals or couples while they were in motion and sell them the photos there and then.

* * *

Don Francisco's grandfather, el Conde de Garvey, had made a fortune from sherry: a fashionable aperitif in rich houses around the world. In 1910 he became wealthy enough to buy the royal hunting ground of the Coto Donaña, which included the Marismas marshland, at the estuary of the river Guadalquiver. Birds sought sanctuary there on their migratory journeys. We spent weekends at the Coto Doñana, travelling together *en famille* in a bus-like vehicle, speeding along empty roads in the dry landscape, past the wayside hoardings advertising sherry produce: the black silhouette of the *toro de Osborne*, fourteen metres high, would appear against the skyline on one of the low hill tops, as well as the *Don* sign of Sandeman; a shadowy *caballero de Jerez* dressed in cape and hat.

> We played "I spy".
> *Veo, veo.*
> *¿Que ves?*
> *Una cosa.*
> *¿Que cosa?*
> *Maravillosa*
> *¿De que color ?*
> *Verde…que te quiero verde*
>
> I see, I see.
> What do you see?
> Something.
> What thing?

> Something marvellous.
> What colour is it ?
> Green. I love you green.

It was at the Coto Doñana that the girls taught me to sing *Sevillanas*. Rhymes fitting perfectly with the tunes, melody picked up from the previous lines and repeated in a three-part perfect *copla* of springy, decisive rhythm – always repeating itself and always ending abruptly;

> *Ar-en-al de Sev-ill-a **y o-lé***
> *Tor-re del Or-o.*
> *Torre del Oro*
> *Arenal de Sevilla*
> *olé torre del oro*
> *Donde los Sevillanos y olé*
> *juegan al toro*
>
> Arenal de Sevilla and olé
> Golden Tower.
> Golden Tower
> Arenal de Sevilla
> Olé Golden Tower
> Where Sevillian people
> Play at bullfighting

Those of us present joined in. We invented percussion with *palmas*, hand-clapping, and *pica*s, finger snapping as well as foot stamping – *zapateo*. The girls danced with raised arms, weaving in and out of each other, making Sevillanas their own.

We sang songs about the sun and the moon and gypsy tales of love, which too often ended in tragedy. The raggle taggle gypsies were part of Irish folklore too, but people were closer to gypsies in Andalusia. Gypsies were instantly recognisable, the men as slim as girls with silky long hair. They lived on the outskirts of towns and cities, like Jerez, Sevilla and Granada.

I could well understand why a girl would want to escape from the kind of house where we lived – where there wasn't even a garden or a patio and the only daylight was on the roof top – and run away with a gypsy. A gypsy was just slightly more mortal than a fairy to my mind. A girl could escape to the mountains of Granada and live a night time existence, under the moon and the stars.

One girl died of love when her gypsy lover didn't return. Her corpse was green when she emerged from the water, like Hamlet's Ophelia. The dead girl gazed at the world with unseeing cold silver eyes.

Verde que te quiero verde
verde carne, pelo verde
con ojos de fría plata.
Las cosas la están mirando
y ella no puede mirarlas

Green I love you green,
green flesh, green hair,
with eyes of cold silver.
Things are looking at her
And she can't look at them.

The sun, the moon and stars had personalities in poems and songs and creatures could feel sad or glad in verses. A story about a married couple of lizards growing old was very moving. They had lost their little iron wedding rings and were saddened by the passing of time from which there was no escape.

> *El lagarto está llorando*
> *La lagarta está llorando*
> *El Lagarto y la lagarta*
> *con delantalitos blancos.*
> *Han perdido sin querer su anillo de desposados*
> *¡Ay su anillito de plomo*
> *¡Ay su anillito plomado!*
> *¡Mirad los, que viejos son!*
> *¡Que viejos son los lagartos!*
> *¡Ay cómo lloran, y lloran!*
> *¡ay, ay como están llorando!*

With such meter and repetition in the songs and verses, I learnt the language step by step – *copla* by *copla*. He cries, she cries. They wear little white aprons. They lost their wedding ring without meaning to: their little ring of lead, their little leaden ring. Look at them! They are so old. The lizards are old. How they cry and cry, how they are crying.

* * *

'Let's go down to the shore ' the *niñas* always said as soon as we arrived at the Coto Doñana. We ran down to the beaches to watch as the great migration of birds arrived from Africa: armies of pink flamingos touching down at the mouth of the river Guadalquivir. They stood one-legged, asleep in the water, or grazed the sandy bottom of the river, scooping up shrimps with broken-shaped beaks to refresh their startling pinkness. Sometimes they danced, all of one mind in a flock, swaying first in one direction and then in the other.

With the *niñas mayores*, I learnt to ride side-saddle after a fashion. I was unhappy in the saddle and always got a stitch sitting on the old nag selected for me. I didn't like the way it looked over its shoulder, chewing the reins with large yellow teeth and trying to bite me. Once I saw a neatly camouflaged lynx, with whiskered ears and spotted fur, hiding out in the dappled shade of an evergreen oak tree.

When there was a big hunting party at the Palacio de las Marismillas, we had to keep out of the way. We ate in the kitchen and kept away from the dining room, where the mounted heads of animals from previous hunts watched from the walls as hunters ate gamey dishes at an enormous table with gusto – *con gusto*.

Once, the Royal Family of Spain in exile came to the Coto Doñana from Portugal for a hunting weekend. Those who had been present described how they had looked down from the gallery of the dining room to see the young prince Juan Carlos and the infantas, Pilar and blind Margarita. They were an unfortunate family that lived outside Spain for political reasons. Don Francisco thought they might be allowed to return one day, if it suited General Franco. Maybe they would get back their confiscated palaces and parks. There had been a personal tragedy as well. Juan Carlos, the boy seen from the balcony, had shot his brother Alfonso by mistake in a hunting accident. **He had shot his own brother dead by mistake!** How could that possibly happen?

After one big game hunt, we *niñas* viewed the bloody corpses of wild boar; dozens of them lined up outside the lodge, waiting to be skinned and butchered. We cringed at the sight of so much death. As well as being a nature reserve, the Coto Doñana was a place for killing animals. The hunters told us not to worry. It was necessary to cull the boar to keep numbers down. Also, it was a good thing for another reason, as the meat would be distributed *"a los pobres"*.

Chapter Seven

In full summer, when Jerez was unfit for human habitation, only the most decrepit of retainers, those too old to leave the house, remained within the walls of the Palacio Garvey and endured the heat under the roof top rooms of the *azotea*.

The rest of us escaped, the household moving first westwards to Extremadura, before heading north, to end up by the cool Atlantic coast of the Basque country in August.

Before leaving, I met with Javier at Los Cisnes. He said he would be waiting anxiously for my return and we would resume our friendship after the holidays. His last letter before we left said:

> *I want to remember what you are like – all parts of you – so that the time will pass quickly when you are away.*

* * *

It was just as hot in Extremadura as it was in Jerez, but at least there we could spend time out of doors. We occupied a rural hunting lodge in a small hamlet at the head of a horseshoe of buildings. To one side a simple church had been constructed. An area of swept mud served as a plaza. Some twenty families lived in the humble houses around the plaza.

The men in the community worked the land, stripping the bark from the cork trees of an ancient forest, which stretched for miles. They cared for the sheep that grazed there. The little shepherd children never went to school.

It hardly ever rained. The women drew water in buckets from a deep well, which they carried to their houses for cooking and cleaning. They sprinkled precious well water on the ground to lay the dust.

Doña Mariana came with bundles of outgrown clothes and garments produced at her knitting machine. She doled them out ceremoniously to the mothers and children.

We *niñas* were allowed to spend time with the estate girls and boys. They showed us the secrets of the countryside: where a stork was nesting, or the place where wild boar scratched their backsides, and where to find wild fruit. Once we found a scorpion under a stone.

'It likes to hide in the daytime,' said Blanca.

It looked like a not-so-small lobster with big nippers. It had the same carapace. Would I die from its sting? I asked. You surely would, they said, trying to frighten me.

'You see that its tail is segmented into five yellow lengths,' said Blanca, who was interested in science. 'The sixth segment is curled up and delivers a strong venom. The sting is very painful. It might not kill you, a healthy person, but a baby or a dog would be in danger.'

For our entertainment, the country children set fire to a ring of kerosene they had poured around the poor beast. The scorpion searched for an escape route and failing to find a way out, struck frantically with its tail on the ground in an attempt to sting. Then it looked like it was stabbing itself repeatedly from the arrow-sharp tail. Minutes passed before it ended its dance of death to curl up and die.

That summer there was a special event to celebrate; a young man from the estate had completed his studies for the priesthood. He had been sent to a seminary at the age of twelve. Now, fourteen years of study later, he would celebrate his first mass in the presence of his benefactors.

A congregation of fifty or so people attended. The priest's family were there: parents, siblings, cousins. Children dressed in the recently donated, freshly laundered clothes carried posies of jasmine.

The church had just been whitewashed and sunlight streaming through the windows bounced off the brightest of walls, giving clarity to the occasion. The young priest's every gesture was slow and deliberate, made meaningful by the newness to him of the ritual. His hands articulating the consecration and distributing the host in communion were soft and his nails were scrubbed clean, in contrast to those of his land-working kinsmen in the congregation receiving the sacrament. I could see the layers of clothing – the white alb tunic worn over his normal clothes and under the gold-embroidered chasuble: all vestments borrowed especially for the celebration from the parish church in the nearby town of Naval Moral de la Mata. When the new *pastor* of men – he had previously been a *pastor* of sheep – prostrated himself before the rustic altar, I saw that the leather soles of his shoes had small inset circles of careful mending. In the sermon the new priest paid homage to his patrons. He thanked them for making it possible for him to fulfil his vocation. He thanked his old parents for bringing him up to be God-fearing. Afterwards, the priest and members of his family kissed Don Francisco's hands as they filed past him at the door.

* * *

A baby was born in the village. We *niñas* would be allowed to see it after some ten days had passed. The mother was still confined to bed. We waited in the parlour for her to arrange herself before we entered her room. What on earth could she be up to? She looked like an invalid when we were finally admitted. She lay encased in a voluminous white nightgown amid starched sheets on a small double bedstead. I wondered if she was ill and if staying in bed was an inevitable part of childbirth. The baby had profuse black hair and snuffled in her arms. I wanted her to rise up out of this confinement and move about.

Although Ireland was a country of large families, I had not been privy to much childbearing in my life. My mother had been over forty when I was born. My father was so old he had been a veteran of World War 1 and had died when I was nine years old. My married sister was a decade older than I was and had had her babies in hospital. My brother, unmarried, was fifteen years older and felt it his duty to take a parental stance in my regard, so such matters were never discussed, neither did he have any children. Only in Spain did I come across women giving birth, which they did at home in secrecy, surrounded by female relatives. I had watched Doña Mariana during her pregnancy in the dark rooms of the second floor of the Palacio Garvey, with only Dolores to comfort her. She had disappeared to be with her mother as the time of the birth drew near, reappearing some time later to hand over her baby to Tata.

At school in Dublin we had been taught that life was a Vale of Tears and women especially were born to suffer and bring forth children in agony. Everything I had seen and intuited so far bore this theory out. I didn't think I would ever want to join the ranks of childbearing women.

Chapter Eight

After the spell in Extremadura, the household moved north, to the temperate Basque country, where it rained (normal weather for me) and greenery abounded. We took up residence in a villa with gardens overlooking the sea. I was still *"muy gorda"* although no longer anaemic, It depressed me that I had only served five months of my two year stretch in Spain, but at least I was now nearer home – just across the sea from my own Dublin Bay. I wondered how everyone was getting on at home and whether I was still remembered. There was no sign that I was. I had sent my Basque address to a few friends in case anyone was interested, in case they should find themselves in the region so they could bring me news. But I half hoped no one would come and discover how much I had changed.

Paul, who lived and worked in London, did try to keep in touch with me. He sent me books – stories by the Russian writers Turgenev and Chekov to keep me company. Ma sent me an occasional letter covering both sides of a blue Basildon Bond sheet. I always held it up to the light to see the reassuring watermark. Her missives did not vary much in content – just a few lines about family and neighbours – but I was glad just to have the physical letter and to see her big handwriting on the page. I could tell how she was by her handwriting, whether her hand was firm or wobbly.

> *Dear Steph,*
> *We are freezing cold here and you are lucky to be in the sun. Rose and Dennis came with the children for Sunday lunch. I cooked a rib of rare beef, the way you like it. Also, my jam tarts were well received as usual.*
> *The children want to know what you will bring them back from Spain when you come. I told them you wouldn't be back for ages and they couldn't understand why their auntie had left them to go so far away. They have no babysitter now, as any stranger would expect to be paid. They really like the postcards you send, especially the ones with the frilly material attached – the flamenco dresses stuck to the girl drawn on the paper.*
> *Paul is planning to visit you in Spain soon.*
> *The tide is very high at the moment and twice came up over the sea wall on to the railway line.*
> *I miss you my little friend. There is no one to bring me tea in the mornings.*
> *I hope you are behaving yourself?*
> *Love from Mamma.*

I would reply on the separate white sheets of notepaper I had bought at the *papelería* – more like fabric material than paper – with matching envelopes.

But despite my efforts to remain in contact, nobody ever responded to the details of what I wrote. My words sank into a void. The members of my family were too taken up with their own affairs. They didn't try to understand what life might be like for me. I didn't know how they imagined a foreign place to be or what they thought my role might be. I had become a non-person, dislocated and unappreciated. I didn't exist any more in the place where I should have been.

* * *

We spent our days at the *concha* of Zarauz: a mile long, shell-shaped beach, where the villas of wealthy summer inhabitants were set back from the shore in surrounding gardens. The mature garden of our villa was on different levels. In the evenings we sat on the built-up walls under the pine trees nearest the sea enjoying the cool Atlantic breezes – a relief after so many long days cooped up in the Andaluz house.

The *niñas* spent hours playing Elastic: two of them faced each other with a loop made from several meters of elastic encircling their legs at the ankles. The third girl hopped in and out of the loop, avoiding as far as possible the sting to her legs if she did not clear the pliable material. Or else they would play skipping games, again as a threesome, with two girls holding each end of the rope. I learnt their store of skipping rhymes. I taught them mine – an English rhyme with a gypsy theme, which I thought appropriate for Spain.

> My mother told me I never should
> play with the gypsies in the wood.

> If I did, she would say
> naughty little girl to disobey.
> Disobey. Disobey.
> Naughty little girl to disobey.

One day I was skulking behind the dunes, reading, when Pepa came running from the house to bring me a message.

'There is someone to see you,' she said. 'Someone from Ireland.'

My thoughts turned to Ma. I worried about her, her dreadful cough. But she would be better now in summer, I thought. The bronchitis, which exacerbated her emphysema, only laid her low in winter. It must be an emissary. She had sent someone to check up on me. Maybe it was my brother Paul – or worse, one of my school friends? Oh God, I thought. Let me not be seen in this state. Word will get back to Dublin that I am a fat pig. Who could be waiting for me in the drawing room of the villa? It was dark in the room entering from the blinding light outside and it took me a moment to realise that it was Michael emerging from the shade. Michael, my best and only friend was fulfilling his promise to visit me in Spain.

We had made grand plans to meet up on the days we spent glued together down on the sea wall. Sixteen-year-old Michael had travelled all this way to find me. And here I was, transformed by captivity, my sad heart concealed under layers of blubber.

'Let's go to the beach,' he said, seeming unfazed by my appearance. The beach was our natural environment. The

Atlantic ocean of the Basque country was the same sea that beat the shores of Dublin Bay with which we were both so familiar. There we could relax, be more at home. But we weren't going anywhere. Doña Mariana had heard about the visit and barged into the room. 'María Antonia is waiting for you,' she said. 'Your friend can have some lunch with you here and afterwards he must leave.'

Pepa bustled in to set up a card table for the two of us. We sat awkwardly face to face. Pepa served *cocido* – the chickpea stew with lumps of gristle I hated. Michael talked about his journey, how it had been very easy hitchhiking through Europe. He had found me according to directions given, with no trouble. I was so sorry he had come. I had exaggerated in my letters home, conveying a positive vision of a glamorous existence. I had promised introductions and a bed at the Garvey establishment to anyone who had the initiative to find me. In truth I was alone and forlorn. I could not offer hospitality to anyone. I wanted to unburden myself, tell Michael how lonely I was and beg him to take me away with him when he left. He would have been horrified had I done so. It dawned on me even then that I would never be able to pick up the threads of my Dublin life. Even if Ma stayed there and didn't move to London to be nearer to Paul as she threatened to do. How would I attach myself again? Get a grip on my lost world? I didn't even have a school to go back to.

We finished our *postre* and then it was time for Michael to leave.

He said he understood that his visit was unacceptable to the family as they were so old fashioned. It couldn't be helped. He said that I shouldn't feel bad that he had not been welcomed. But I felt guilty that he had wasted his time coming to see me. I was powerless to make it up to him. He said he would be fine and would take a look at San Sebástián before returning to Dublin. I watched him walk away from the house with his knapsack on his back. He was upright, fresh-faced, and free.

Chapter Nine

The incident with Michael embittered me. It showed that I could never live my own life. I was trapped. I had no place to be. I was alone and no one cared what I thought or said. I had probably been sent away from Dublin because of Michael anyway, and I didn't think I would ever see him again.

He and I had had only a fragile, tentative closeness. At first I couldn't understand why he was hanging around. Ma was not worried when she saw him, as by that time she had given up on being an effective disciplinarian. She had lowered her standards after my brother and sister left home and after five years as a widow. Michael would suddenly appear and we would go off together. He wasn't like the other boys and didn't care about football or the weekend rugby matches at Landsdowne Road. Instead he came to see me. We talked about books we came across. We read the Russian writers and we knew some verse – the single aspect of Irish education that got through to the pupils. We could all recite Yeats: "Come Away, O human child!" and Thomas Hood:

"I remember, I remember the house where I was born the little window where the sun came peeping in at dawn."

Michael said he wanted to be a forester and live an outdoor life. He told me not to worry when it transpired I had to go to Spain. He said he would come and find me there.

He had come all that way just to see me and had been sent away without ceremony. That would never happen in Dublin, I thought, or certainly not in our house, where everyone was welcome. We had open house every Sunday when Paul was a student at Trinity College. Foreigners were especially welcome to our soirées. We were curious about their ways. We really wanted to know what other people thought. We wanted to learn their languages. We exchanged poetry and sang songs with our visitors. Why was it not the same in the Garvey household?

My employers had made me sever another of my tenuous links with home. I couldn't believe the injustice. The incident shocked me out of my lethargy and curtailed my obsession with food. I determined not to be so passive and vowed that I would not eat my way through the rest of my days in Jerez de la Frontera. I would care for my appearance. I would go to the dressmaker with my pocket money and have new dresses made – even though I would have to hide them, as the women of the household were so strict about modes of dressing: skirt hems below the knee, no short sleeves and nothing tight.

In September, we returned to Jerez de la Frontera in time for the start of the new term. I missed the girls when they went back to school, having grown used to their companionship during the long holiday. I was again left to my own devices with only a slightly improved situation. At least I had become familiar with the *piropo* and grown used to the youths, and often grown men, who stuck their faces into mine as I stepped out with Señorita. I wasn't so bothered by their attentions and ignored the workmen who said I was the queen of their entrails (*tu eres la reina de mis entrañas*) and I scoffed when they offered to eat all parts of me, especially my blooming breasts (*que te como el pecho*). Even though there was always a threat in the *piropo*, I decided not to care.

"*Tetona, culona!*" they would shout, referring to my breasts and bottom. But I had grown indifferent to the taunts and lost my fear of the streets. I even came to accept the beggars with terrible mutilations and defiant stares who demanded *pesetas* on street corners and outside churches. I was no longer shocked by the blind men and women selling lottery tickets, offering the best and luckiest numbers in a singsong voice: "*para hoy, la cincuenta y dos para hoy*." I still couldn't make out why there were so many "*inválidos*", cripples and beggars living on the streets, but I accepted their presence too. Maybe they had all been in the wars, I thought. There had to be an explanation for the sheer numbers. Dirty little children seemed to have suffered terrible accidents. Often limbless, they sat by their plates blaspheming, shouting out filthy upsetting things.

Imagine a child saying: "*me cago en tu boca*" or "*me cago en Dios*". *Cagar* was a verb I could never bring myself to say. Nobody mentioned "shit" in Dublin – not as a noun and certainly not as a verb. I had never heard the word said by anyone in my whole life, and to say it in the same breath as a prayer to God was extremely unsettling. They would say "*hostias*" too, which I was horrified to learn meant the Sacred Host of Holy Communion. Spain was certainly a different world. I didn't know how people got away with the things they said. No such breech of the rules of politeness would be tolerated in Ireland. "Wash your mouth out with soap" we would be told for the slightest deviation from courteous speech.

Another improvement in my life after the holidays was an exchange of Señoritas for my sorties downtown, which always had to be accompanied by somebody. Pilar was the Señorita of the household of Doña Mariana's older sister, Doña Mati, who was married to Pedro Domecq, breeder of the best bulls in the province of Cadiz and – apart from the houses of Gonzalez Byass and Williams and Humbert – the most successful exporter of sherry. Mati had nine children.

I found Pilar to be a more understanding companion. At thirty-four, she was double my age, the same age as Javier. Due to her lack of family fortune and lowly position in the Domecq household, she was considered to be without marriage prospects locally, but she was much more glamorous than our señorita. Pilar and I negotiated with Doña Mati and Doña Mariana. They could not deny our occasional meetings and *merienda* at the hotel Los Cisnes. Apart from the evening *paseo* with the girls, this was my only recreation and break from the household.

I was quite looking forward to seeing Javier again and maybe we would continue our interrupted correspondence.

'You may go with Pilar,' said Doña Mariana. 'But remember

that your standards of behaviour must be beyond criticism. Perhaps you will meet other boys and girls from Ireland there. I know you are lonely, but we have our reputation to consider and it is not good for members of the household to be seen in public places.'

I didn't remind her that she had already sent away my friend from Ireland, who happened to be a boy, and so it was unlikely that she would approve of any other boy, so obviously she meant I could only find a girl to be my friend. She didn't know about Javier. Would she approve of him?

* * *

A task was found to help me fill in the days. This was reading the novels of Charles Dickens or Jane Austen to the blind Marqués. Typically I would be summoned in the early afternoon to the formally furnished, dark sitting room where he sat in an upright, winged-upholstered armchair. I could be there for several hours. The Marqués was taciturn. He wore pink-tinted spectacles and had a tartan rug over his knees even on warm days. Communication was difficult; either he was deaf, or too old to make an effort, or else he thought I was a servant and he didn't communicate with servants, or else he had always been reserved and shy. Whatever the case, it was difficult getting through to him.

I began to read. I couldn't tell if he followed the words or not from the expression on his face. He never laughed at the funny bits. He wasn't caught up in the drama, as we would be in Dublin, where reading aloud was a favourite pastime and an element of our weekend soirées at home. I wondered if he appreciated the kind and wealthy gentleman that was Mister Samuel Pickwick, Esquire, and the London sayings of the time in the words of his sidekick, Sam Weller? Did he understand the ridiculous adventures of Pickwick Club members? Did he appreciate the jokes? I suspected he was not in the least bit interested in the London of Charles Dickens, any more than he cared about the Pump Room at Bath when we read Jane Austen. We began the session by remembering where we had left off on the previous occasion. At intervals I stopped reading to see if he was asleep, as he nodded off as soon as I established a rhythm with my voice. I would stop and count under my breath for a considerable interval before loudly clearing my throat, until he stirred and often sighed. In halting English, he asked me to recap whenever he woke up, which I did, and then I would read on, stopping and starting; the same routine over and over again. Sometimes his breathing slowed right down and I imagined he had died while I read. This was quite likely as, given the situation, I too was dying of boredom.

Chapter Ten

The hotel Los Cisnes was the favoured meeting place in Jerez de la Frontera on the Calle José Antonio (later to be renamed the *Calle Larga*). The panelled bar, which had a full-length wrought-iron interior screen, was well attended after *siesta* and before the *paseo*. Over sweet, viscous cups of hot chocolate, Pilar and I discussed the women in our respective households, the two Sevillian sisters, Mati and Mariana who had made such advantageous marriages. But they really weren't much better off than we were, we decided. Apart from returning to their family home in Sevilla, they never went anywhere alone. Mariana's main form of entertainment was the knitting machine she had been given by her husband so that she could knit similar sweaters in the same colour for all her children and nieces and nephews as well as the children on the Cáceres estate. It had many rows of tiny metal hooks, with a flap over each opening, like small hands, which opened and shut to receive the wool when a counter was passed back and forth to create the rows. She sat in a room never reached by the sun – a bit like the Lady of Shallot – in semi-darkness, mesmerised by the to-ing and fro-ing of the counter in her hands, with only her confidential lady's maid, Dolores, as companion.

At Los Cisnes, I was reacquainted with Javier, who had not written letters to me during the summer months when I was away, but was prepared to fulfil his promise on my return and resume our correspondence. My chaperone, Pilar, wasn't at all bothered by Javier. She didn't consider him predatory and so our friendship proceeded unimpeded. Whenever we met, Javier told me stories and made me laugh. He was not at all threatening, although he had once been a *torero* of promise and had faced danger when confronting the might of the bull. He was anxious to impress and his attachment to me resulted in an increase of my bullfighting vocabulary. Although I had never been to a bullfight, I had been to the Plaza de Toros on the outskirts of town on a visit. There I saw the little chapel, the place where the *diestros* prayed before the *corrida* that their capes would never fail them. I also saw the blue and white tiled plaques erected to the bravest bull from every season, stating from which estate they came. Each one had a pet name, like one might name a dog or a cat: *Chiquilín; Corcito; Compuesto; Velador; Jirivilla*. When there was no brave bull for the torero to fight, only a tame one, the plaque declared the fight a desert, "*desierto*": unworthy and a disgrace to the estate of provenance.

Javier said bullfighting was an art. He demonstrated this by a kind of dance, describing what was involved in *toreando con capa* and the various *faenas* at his disposal, whether approaching the bull from front, back or sideways. He went through these passes so I could fully understand, using a copy of the *Diario de Jerez*, which hung from a stick on a rack, or else a cardigan or jacket to act as a cape. He taught me about *chiquelines* and *verónicas* and the glory in them. He said that at times there was so much danger and tension in the bullring that it was like being in a pressure cooker.

'The pink cape rises to the heavens with all the inspiration, essence and grace of the art,' he explained. A harmony could be achieved when bull and fighter entered into a pact with the public (*el de siempre*) going back in time and engulfing the soul. He explained the solemnity involved in the moment – a sacramental moment – when the bull is given its death. I was captivated by his description and could nearly smell the blood and the sand. Neither of us mentioned the suffering of the poor animal. Javier was nostalgic, always returning to the past. But really these descriptions and his playacting for me at Los Cisnes were all that remained of his past life.

He presented me with photos of himself dressed in his golden "suit of lights" worn with pink stockings and dainty bullfighting pumps. His long hair was scraped back from his forehead to be caught up behind in a little bun. He dedicated his bulls to me warmly, in the present tense, even though the fight had taken place at some distance in the past, indicating that, had he known me at the time, I would have been his choice of person to whom he would dedicate his acts of valour. He told me he had once received two ears, for a clean kill, and had been hoisted aloft on the shoulders of his *compañeros de corrida* to leave the bull ring through the great door – *la puerta grande* – ceremoniously opened for the most heroic.

But that had been at the height of his career in the small town of Arcos de la Frontera and it seemed that one ear was the usual level of his attainment.

We determined to meet when I had a day off, and we would exchange letters in the meantime. I thought this a normal arrangement, one that I was used to, as Javier was the same age as my brother – fifteen years older than I was – and Paul wrote to me all the time. He had never failed to send me regular postcards from France during the year he was a teacher there. He sent me books to Spain and made up poetry for me.

So we corresponded, Javier and I. His letters weren't exactly like Paul's, although, similarly, the missives did not require much return from me. I was the passive recipient for the most part, although he did beg me to write more, but he understood that my written Spanish was not on a par with his. Not yet, anyway. He had so many worries to impart, what he called "*mis penas*" – all to do with not being a good enough bullfighter, not having a good job and not being able to support his mother. He seemed to be making some kind of proposal to me – I couldn't work out what exactly – except that maybe I would whisk him away somewhere and look after him.

I knew misunderstandings were bound to arise as we spoke different languages but, above all, our meanings were different, and that was quite exciting in a way. Javier understood this. One letter read:

> *Querida Estefanía,*
> *Is it true what you say, that you find it difficult to express yourself in Spanish? Even if words are translated I think they lose*

their force and their complete expression, don't you think? Things get half-said, because the one that says and the one that translates cannot arrive at the exact same point of the idea.
  Your friend, Javier

An important difference from the letters from home in Javier's letters was that he mentioned "love" an awful lot – something I wasn't used to. Irish people never talked about love unless it was the love of God.

One way or another I was learning a great deal about Spanish men, what with Francisco sitting on my bed in the evenings for a chat about Madrid and Javier writing me letters and the men at the bar of Los Cisnes plying me with sweet sherry.

I learnt about the women too, but separately; about the girls and their female relatives and the women, both upstairs and downstairs, and I had plenty of time at my disposal to take it all in.

At times I felt quite relaxed in the company I was keeping. But when I did I believed myself to be engaging in disloyalty to my family at home. I was attached to the *niñas* and we played happily together at card games, or a game of rounders at the Casa de Campo. I also enjoyed rediscovering the classic tales of children's literature with them, tales from my recent past that we read together. Despite myself, I was adapting reluctantly to some aspects of Jerez life. I was mixing in and taking local ways for granted.

* * *

Pilar introduced me to her dressmaker, Encarnita, She could copy any model from the German pattern book, *Bunda*. I decided to use my meagre pocket money – six pounds a month – to update my wardrobe. I bought material from the *mercería*, another old-fashioned shop with unusual merchandise: bolts of silk and cotton in colours even Ma would have approved of. Then I scrutinised the stylised, elongated models on the pages of Bunda; carefully noting the lengths of skirt and sleeves as well as necklines before making decisions. What to choose? It was a strange experience, an entirely new sensation to be dressed by somebody else. I was closeted with Encarnita in a curtained, mirrored cubicle as she swathed material around my torso. Concentrating deeply, she sat back on her knees to fix a hem at floor level, her mouth full of pins extracted from the velvet cushion she wore like a bracelet around her wrist. She knew exactly how to measure and shape the cloth to fit. She cut the fabric there and then, tacking the edges together immediately. I examined myself closely in the mirror during these sessions, noting every aspect of my reflection. Over the three necessary fittings which took place before I collected the finished garment, I had ample opportunity to see for myself how I was changing physically, becoming browner and sleeker as the days passed. I hardly recognised myself.

My taste veered towards the flamboyant. I was particularly fond of a flame and cream patterned material, made up as a wrap-around sleeveless dress. My second favourite was a full-skirted, shiny, royal blue dress with a square neckline, which I wore with a hooped petticoat. Encarnita managed the necklines perfectly. She was fussy about the finish and insisted on wide seams – plenty of extra material in case I should need to let the dresses out in the future. She made a zig-zag edge with her pinking shears

Both of these dresses had to be kept hidden from the family. Only Blanca and Fatima saw the clothes I had in my wardrobe. Usually I wore a plain skirt and blouse. I thought it might be said that my new clothes were unsuitable, particularly as they showed my arms. Already, to my great embarrassment, I had been asked to leave the church of Santo Domingo because of wearing a sleeveless dress. The rules governing what women wore in church were very strict: covered arms and no bare legs, stockings and long skirts at all times for *señoras* – no matter how hot the day – and socks for girls. A black lace head triangle with the peak at the front was an essential item of clothing to be carried at all times, in case an occasion for church visiting arose. If one forgot this, it was necessary to improvise with a handkerchief – a gesture towards head covering. In Sevilla, I once saw a woman in a long black dress wearing a full-length mantilla: yards of lace dropping from a high tortoise-shell comb to below the knee. There were white ones for weddings.

Chapter Eleven

Today I told mamma that I have an Irish girlfriend and she is enchanting. She said to me – half serious, half joking, "See if that girl can straighten out your head and make you more satisfied with your lot in life." I also told her that when I go abroad she needn't be worried because at least I'll have good friends – your friends – so I will not be alone.

She thinks I am only going away to have a good time and she worries. I tell her that if I go with only enough money for the journey, how can I have a good time? If I find myself in difficulties, I'll come straight back to Jerez. I want to work. I don't care what work. I tell her that my objective is to learn English, which I would never learn here, and she knows that I am a good boy. It's just that I have these fantasies.

In the end she is convinced. She tells me that I have a heart of gold and says if it helps me to forget my worries then I should go, but she wants me to have guaranteed employment. Then she gets a little bit sad, but when my brothers are here she is more at peace. Before knowing you, a friend wrote to me from Paris, telling me what I should do, but I know nothing of that place. I dream of London, I think England is better that France, I don't know why. I have the impression of repeating myself. Do I? If I do, forgive me.

I've always had a horror of being a bore. When I ring you today at 2.30, will you still be reading my letter?

Javier hoped to leave Jerez one day. He imagined I would help him. He didn't seem to be very good at making plans. It was as if he was trying to hand over responsibility for his future to me; plant an idea in my mind to be responsible for him. The subject cropped up every so often in his letters, before he switched to his other favourite topic: love!

> *Something you say in your letter that I don't understand although I think I know what it is. You say, "I wouldn't be Spanish even if I could be." I didn't quite understand what you meant by that but I'll explain what I think and hope you understand me. Whether you were Chinese, Greek, Indian or whatever, I would have fallen in love with you. That's all. Of course if you weren't what you are you wouldn't have those eyes, that hair and that complexion and, above all, that air about you and those physical attributes that God gave you. I like you because you are Stefanie and that's all I know. Do you understand me?*
>
> *You have something that attracts me. I think it's called IMAN, or electrons, bewitchery, duende and all that. It's a force that attracts me to you!*

Javier wrote a great deal – pages and pages in small tight writing. He told me about some aspects of his life: about his relationship with his mother, about his inability to settle down, about his past failures, but above all about his desire to go abroad. He also paid me compliments and declared an infatuation. He did not tell me why he was still living with his mamma at his ripe age. He did not tell me what had happened to his father. Nor did he tell me about any previous or present girlfriends. He seemed to be endlessly available – not busy at all. I could see he was a dreamer and I liked that side of him.

Out of boredom and also because I didn't want to appear impolite, I responded dutifully – consulting my small Collins dictionary – penning my replies and taking them regularly to deposit in the yellow Correos post-box.

Sometimes, when I was given permission to go for a walk, we met at *La Moderna Pastelería,* an old style café and cake shop. We engaged in banter as we drank weak Lipton Tea and ate sweet milk rolls filled with delicate ham, which for some reason were called "midnights" – *medianoches*. We took pleasure in exchanging stories and telling jokes. He taught me words and corrected my Spanish.

I asked him what "*IMAN*" meant.

'It is a Moorish word', he said. 'It is something wonderful, as when the butterfly emerges from the chrysalis. You are only a girl but you will be a woman soon and that change is happening to you now.'

'What's the word in Spanish for that?'

'Nothing, there isn't a word, and that's why we use a Moorish word. The Spanish language has many, many Arabic words because you know we are really Moors. Yes, we are *Moros* … even though we are very Catholic people and we kicked the Moors out because of their Mohammedan religion. We kicked the Jews out too. But all these people left their blood behind when they were expelled from Spain: their blood and their language, their gardens and their songs, and we live at the frontier of their lands in these villages and towns of the Frontera: Jerez de la Frontera, Arcos de la Frontera, Vejer de la Frontera. We grow their food: olives, pomegranates and *chirimoya* (a heart-shaped fruit with big black pips and green dappled skin and cream flesh, which tasted like bananas and cream when eaten with a teaspoon). 'We eat oranges and lemons from their trees and make cakes from their honey and almonds. We irrigate our vegetables with their waterways – channels running down the terraces to catch the melting snow from the sierra.'

And then Javier would say I was trying to avoid him, that I didn't care about him enough and he would sing me a Sevillana:

Porque no veniste, amor
Esta noche, la pasada.
Estaba la noche clara
Y el caminito andador
sabiendo que te esperaba…..

Why didn't you come, love,
this last night?
The night was clear
and the pathway well-lit for you to come,
knowing I was waiting.

Chapter Twelve

Another person looking for an adventure abroad was Pilar. Like Javier, she listened avidly when I spoke of home, which I did a great deal to anyone who would listen. I embroidered my place of origin. I told them about our flat at 99 Seapoint Avenue, Monkstown, with its imposing stone lions guarding the front door at the top of the sweep of steps. If I closed my eyes I could transport myself back there, to our lofty front room, which Ma called the drawing room, always flooded in light from the bay window looking out over Dublin Bay. This was in stark contrast to the dark rooms of Spain, with everyone escaping into the centre of buildings, far from the blistering sun. I spoke of my wonderful writer brother, Paul, who they would surely love as I did. I spoke of my elder sister, Rose, and her two children to whom I was very attached. I told Blanca and Fatima about my life in Dublin and made up stories about my schooldays to entertain them. I made them laugh by impersonating the nuns at my convent, embellishing personalities for them.

I said I had a collection of very precious dolls from all

parts of the world – far superior to theirs – and that these were invaluable, certainly invaluable to me.

As Christmas drew near, Pilar decided it was time for me to go home and see my mother. In truth I did want to see her but it was Pilar who decided, because she wanted to come with me, being set on an adventure. Through me, she would make a bid to escape the stultifying hierarchy, which trapped women into subservience in Andalusía. Although Javier was not a woman, he was also trapped and desperate to leave Jerez. He imagined I could help him get away as he had no prospects and lived with his widowed mother, who he was supposed to be supporting. However, it would have looked very odd if I'd turned up in Dublin with Javier. So, for better or for worse, my travel companion for going home would be Pilar.

The only problem for our plan to go to Dublin for Christmas was a lack of funding. Where would we get the money for the journey? I had squandered my monthly peseta wages instead of saving, and the family would only pay for my return journey when I had completed the two-year stay. Ma lived on a small widow's pension provided by my deceased father's place of work. Anyway she would never come up with a contribution, even if she had the means. I would have to borrow ten pounds from somebody else. Pilar, in her determination, came up with the solution: I would say that my mother was ill and I had to go and see her. I would borrow enough money from Doña Mariana to go home by train. On a visit to Sevilla, I borrowed £10 from Rita from my school. I didn't want to be beholden to her but she was the only person I knew with money. She was better at saving than I was, and had squirreled away her allowance instead of buying material at the *mercería* to make frocks. I hated asking Rita and being indebted. She was the wrong person to ask, as I knew she would have a hold over me for evermore, but necessity prevailed.

It wasn't a bad idea to visit home. Ma had not been ill as far as I knew. But then Ma was always sick, suffering as she did from emphysema, brought on by chain-smoking unfiltered Sweet Afton cigarettes. It wouldn't do any harm to go and see her and it would only be half a lie to make an excuse and ask for money.

Chapter Thirteen

After my first experience of flying, I was mortally afraid of aeroplanes. We would have to travel to Dublin by train, which was far cheaper anyway. Doña Mariana agreed to give me an advance on my wages to go and see my sick mother as long as Pilar came with me. Duly chaperoned, I would be allowed to depart from Jerez. In fact Pilar decided not to go by train, so I would be travelling alone. She told me not to tell anyone and arranged for the purchase of train tickets for the Spanish part of my journey. It was not an easy matter to obtain tickets, she said. It wasn't easy to leave Spain at all but as I had a passport and was known to the Guardia from my three monthly visits, I would be able to go home for compassionate reasons and come back. Pilar would make her own way by air to Dublin. We would meet there.

Leaving from the *Estación de Ferrocarril* in Jerez, it took me five days to reach my destination. A cheap third-class steam train, it made its way northwards slowly, continually stopping and starting. We were often diverted into a siding to wait while repairs to the worn out tracks were carried out. I occupied a narrow wooden third-class seat. My knees touched the passenger I faced.

At every station country people clawed their way on board to pack the carriages with their belongings, including baskets of live poultry. We sat jammed together, sharing the pitiful space of thick hot air. The night resounded with snores and groans, the wailing of babies and the crowing of animals.

Young men, on leave from the *mili,* hopped on and off. After the first day, I was heartily sick of the *piropo* – the aggressive propositioning from which there was no escape. I was not looking my best but was nevertheless the object of constant attention because I was alone, young, and foreign. I really felt the need of a chaperone then. There was a lot to be said for the system, certainly necessary in Spain. Why had I allowed Pilar to travel by plane, leaving me to fend for myself?

I hadn't realised that I needed to take food for the journey and was unprepared. Once, a woman gave me a share of her tortilla sandwich, but in the main I was forced to get food and water on the platforms of the many stations where we stopped, buying bread and tomatoes and dried paprika *chorizo* from hawkers. Although I avoided the crude offal stews, the Spanish version of tripe and onions, just the sight of which made me sick to the stomach, I soon became ill with diarrhoea. Bodies and baggage blocked the corridor to the lavatory so for most of the journey and to avoid an accident, I remained standing outside the fetid space which served as the unspeakable WC – always blocked and overflowing; always occupied. The same old man, or perhaps a different one, emerged time and again, fiddling with his fly.

I discarded my guts over and over again on that train. I lowered the window with the leather belt strap so as to get some air and survive. In between bouts of sickness, I returned to my wooden seat and slept fitfully. I dreamt I was carried off and dumped on a rubbish heap, leaking from every orifice, while the locals stood around tut-tutting and saying how *gorda* I was and what was I doing in Spain anyway. *¿Qué hace aqúi la niña? ¿Porque no está en su casa?* Why isn't that girl at home with her family?

As we progressed northwards through the bare uplands of Castille, the pestering diminished. I negotiated changing trains and tickets at the Pyrenean border and was left alone on a better train in France. I crossed on the ferry over the English Channel without incident. My brother Paul saw me safely across London to board the boat train from Euston; then across the Irish Sea to Dublin on the miserable Princess Maud, that dreadful ferry boat, just as bad as any Spanish train.

The Princess Maud heaved and rolled across the Irish Sea. Foul-mouthed labourers returning from the building sites of England packed the bars and there was nowhere to sit. As the alcohol took hold and the sea got rougher, the passageways became slimy with vomit. The only escape was to stand shivering on the deck, gulping down breaths of cold, damp air. I took the punishment meted out. It was my own fault that I found myself in such situations. I could never get things right. I never stayed put long enough to sort myself out. I could not rely on anyone to help me.

* * *

Back in Dublin, Ma was glad to see me. I saw Rose and my little niece and nephew. The members of my family were amazed to see the sheen of good health I had developed once I recovered from the journey. I had always been more than usually skinny but now they said I was like a plump turkey that had been fattened up for Christmas. Three square Spanish meals a day had had a dramatic effect on my person.

I found everything was just as I remembered from far away: the coast road from Seapoint to Sandycove unchanged, the Purty Kitchen pub, the two piers stretching their arms around the sheltered bay for sailing boats; Dun Laoghaire Baths and along to Sandycove Baths. The rocks and seaside shrubs of my childhood were still in place on Marine Parade, from where our gang of girls used to jump out on to the road to give drivers a fright, as they imagined they had run us over.

Ma had kept everything as it was. Nothing had changed in my bedroom – a partitioned corner of Ma's bedroom. My ballet dancer pictures were still tacked to the wall, as well as my pictures of horses and my best souvenir programmes from shows I'd been to at the Olympia Theatre.

Paul came from London. I hoped I would make a good impression on him with my newly acquired linguistic attainments. I hoped he would make a good impression on my glamorous friend, Pilar, soon to appear in Dublin.

Pilar came. She liked what she saw. Everyone made a fuss of her and people we knew queued up to take her out or invite her home. They liked her tanned skin and the peroxide streak in her brown hair. She was an exotic specimen in Ireland, as I was in Spain. But she was much older and utterly ruthless, whereas I was a babe in arms – an Irish waif. She came with a well-thought-out plan, which she proceeded to execute. She would not be returning to Jerez de la Frontera. Before I left Dublin again, she had found a situation as an *au pair* and she settled in. In the long term she will have found the husband she sought, but I lost sight of her. She disappeared not to be seen by me again – neither in Dublin nor Jerez de la Frontera.

It soon became apparent that I had made a mistake by returning to Dublin before my time was up in Spain. I had already left the place of my birth in spirit. I had also romanticised my home life to such a degree that I was unable to believe that none of what I willed my life to be like was true. Nobody – except for Ma, whose life was anyway easier without me – wanted to see me before I was due back. My wonderfully honed linguistic skills were unappreciated. When I rattled away in Spanish, I was accused of showing off. No one cared when I sang my Christmas carol; about the dark-haired Virgin Mary dreaming as she washed her shivering son's little lambskin coat while Saint Joseph fed the fire with little sticks, because it kept going out, due to the cold and the wind and the fog.

La virgen morena
soñaba lavando,
un abrigito de piel de cordero
p'al niño chiquito que esta tiritando.

I thought of refusing to return to Spain. I could just admit defeat and tell Ma that she was asking too much to expect me to stay the course. But I couldn't bear the idea of going back to my previous life. Anyway, we were not in the habit of exchanging personal information about feelings. That was not in the nature of our way of being. I understood that I must not be a nuisance. I had to go away again because there was nothing for me at home. I could not stay at home to watch Ma doing nothing. I would go so that Ma could do nothing in peace. I didn't risk making contact with Michael. He would not have expected to see me and by now he must have a new life without me. I would sneak away again without making a fuss and finish what I had set out to do.

Chapter Fourteen

When I eventually got back to Jerez de la Frontera following the same endless route it was hard to adapt for a second time. I had made myself sad all over again by undertaking the journey, and I had a presentiment that perhaps I would never return home to Dublin again if Ma decided to join Paul in London. This was cause for anxiety. She and I had been happy in her light, airy flat overlooking Dublin Bay. Although we had very few material possessions, we lived in an imposing house with an uninterrupted sea view. We could read the weather from our big sash window by looking directly over the expanse of water to the hill of Howth Head. When the hill appeared up close and clear it would rain, if it was far away and misty we would have good weather. I could cross the road and descend to the built-up rocky bathing place whenever I wanted to swim in summer. There was always someone to chat to there. Once, I met a large, red-faced, fat man, who entertained me with stories in a broad Dublin accent. I was wearing school uniform and he chided me for not going to school. Later, I realised that I had whiled away an hour or two with the great writer, Brendan Behan, who was sunbathing and fortifying himself with bottles of Guinness standing up straight in ranks beside him on the rocks.

We were never alone at Seapoint Avenue. We only had to step out into the communal hall to catch up with the news. That's why I was so lonely in Jerez where people didn't mix in the same way. They stayed in their groups, divided by age or the work they did. I didn't belong to any group. I was not admitted to any circle. I was even a stranger to the girls I lived with. But on my return after that Christmas I was at least more familiar with my surroundings. I could find my way from the Palacio Garvey to the Calle Jose Antonio: past the Gallo Azul Domecq building, with the rounded front and clock face, to eventually arrive at the Hotel Los Cisnes. I was also more confident at expressing myself in Spanish. I decided to do without a chaperone, if the occasion arose. I could manage perfectly well on my own on the shorter walks.

* * *

I had carried back the dolls of my childhood to give to the girls. I thought them an exotic offering and indeed they were. The Japanese doll had long celluloid legs and a swatch of real human hair stuck on to her basket coolie hat rather than her head. The Breton doll wore a lace cap on her nylon hair and her cream water-silk crinoline was encrusted with sequins and beads. Other dolls from exotic places reflected the travels of their donors – mainly my brother, Paul. My favourite though, was not exotic but a fat baby doll called Hazel. She was bald but could open and shut her eyes. She had a rosebud mouth with a hole in the middle from whence a plastic tube ran through to an orifice at the front of her bottom. In my girlhood – up to perhaps twelve years old – I would feed the doll from a miniature bottle of water and change her nappy when the water came out at the other end. If her stomach was squeezed enough, a small bleat could be heard and one could believe she uttered the word "mamma". Hazel had a wardrobe of motley garments for both winter and summer. Ma and various friends of hers had knitted these out of pity for the child whose father had recently died after a shockingly short illness. One moment he was with us and then he was not – a blood vessel had burst in his head and he was carried away. Our friends and neighbours were doubly sympathetic because we had had to move out of our rented house because of our loss of income. An auction was held to dispose of our furniture and other goods. I watched from a neighbour's house as familiar pieces of furniture were carted away by those seeking a bargain. Ma only kept the most valuable bits and pieces which she would take to a new life. My dolls had survived eviction, and provided comfort during the interim period between leaving my childhood home and going to Spain. Now I was giving them away. I minded most about giving up Hazel. But it was to be a radical, all or nothing gesture, and so I parted with the last remnants of my childhood voluntarily and handed over the dolls. After I had parted with these, my only possessions, to Blanca and

Fatima I was overcome with loss. I wanted to ask for them to be returned, especially as they showed little interest in either the objects or their provenance, but my circumstances didn't offer the flexibility of a change of mind, so I was stuck with the generous gesture I had made.

Also my life had become complicated because of the lie I had told about Ma's illness. Somehow this had become a cancer that our family was facing. Doña Mariana was sympathetic and always asked me how my mother was keeping, which meant I was compelled to reinforce the fraud. Furthermore, I now owed a vast amount of money to the family – some £30 – to be deducted from my monthly pocket money. I also owed £10 to the sanctimonious Rita in Sevilla.

I realised that all my woes resulted from Pilar's determination to escape from the constraints of female bondage in Jerez de la Frontera. She had successfully extricated herself while I was stuck. As the loan was deducted from my pocket money, I couldn't even amuse myself by buying materials at the *mercería*. I still went there with Tata when she collected the expertly smocked dresses for the *niñas menores* and smocked suits made of the finest viyella for the *niños menores*. But I was getting too old to be locked up with *niñas* and *niños*, whether *menores* or *mayores*.

The family made some concessions and I was allowed a little more leeway. I would have a day off once every two weeks. Besides letters, I would be allowed to make and receive phone calls from the outside world, put through the switchboard in the *portería*, which took internal calls from the other apartments to allow the parents to speak to their children directly, so they could give instructions for day-to-day activities. Pepa would answer the phone on our floor. She would leap to attention, even though nobody could see her. *"Mande,"* she always said. "*A sus órdenes.*" (*Command me – at your orders.*) I thought this a military response, which she said to please the Generalísimo.

Chapter Fifteen

Javier continued to send me letters. He worried that he didn't support his mother enough. Something had happened to his father. I couldn't discover what. I thought maybe he had been one of the "*rojos*" referred to at the servant gatherings of the *azotea*. He wouldn't tell me why his mother had had to bring up three boys on her own or why his father had abandoned the family. Maybe he had been killed – an accident or something? Javier wouldn't say. His brothers had left home. He was unresolved and restless. He was at a loose end, always referring back to his bullfighting days or looking forward to a future away from Jerez de la Frontera. Sometimes, when he was very depressed, he thought he would never get out of Spain, the problem being that he would never qualify for a passport unless there was someone outside to vouch for him. Spain was a prison and you could only get out if you had a lot of money or wealthy relatives. I knew he had secrets in his past and I was curious to find out what these could be, but he wouldn't be pressed.

He decided that we had matters in common – perhaps

because neither of us had a father and we both worried about our mothers. He said we were both restless. In fact we had very little in common. He was still living at home with his mother in his thirties, and I had already left home, ostensibly to earn my living and learn about life – although from the limited perspective of a feudal household in Andalusia. I suspected I was in Jerez to be out of the way of those at home, keeping faith with the unspoken pact of not being a nuisance to my widowed mother.

But I accepted Javier as he was and enjoyed his philosophising and hapless stories. I waited for his letters to be found at the *portería* as they certainly relieved the boredom of the days. I was disappointed not to find one.

> *I never spoke to you of my saintly mother. She is lovely and always has been and still is….*
>
> *She has suffered a lot with us, but with me she went through hell. In her heart of hearts, she wanted me to become a great bullfighter. She always tells me that I abandon everything I start. I'm a bit like you, in that I don't know what I want. I'm incapable of starting a business because it would take up too much time, more time than I am prepared to designate. Also, I'm not capable of being nice to a person I don't like. This character I have is a problem. I'm always dreaming and I'm sorry not to be practical.*
>
> *Ay, about loving you. That's another thing. I would always love you even if we never saw each other again. You are very much inside me. Did you know that?*
>
> *One thing I would like to do is make a film about bullfighting, and you could work with me. Did I tell you that once I was in a*

film in some scenes about bullfighting in Medina Sidonia? The filmmakers said they would send me a copy of the film but they didn't; afterwards I heard the news indirectly that the film had been destroyed. I don't know why. It's all a matter of luck and I hope to have some one day.

It must be difficult for you to understand all this and maybe you'll get bored. I'm afraid of being tedious.

Write to me whenever you want, as soon as possible and as long as you like. It will serve for you to practice your Castilian and at the same time you will amuse me; take me out of myself and away from my worries. Vale?

I'm very lazy about studying English. I don't know a word and that's the case. Tonight I will go and see our friend Patric (is that the spelling?) to continue with plans to see who wants to be responsible for me in the islands. Sometimes I get pessimistic and think I'll never get away. Something must be done!

I think about you a lot, even if you don't believe me or don't want to believe me.

For you, my best thoughts...
I am very happy.
Javier

I answered the letters as best I could, but the more I became involved, the more pressure Javier put on me to take him away. Of course I couldn't take responsibility for him in London. Surely he could see that? I was too young and I could hardly take responsibility for myself, let alone for another human being. Anyway I lived in Dublin – even if we were shortly to move to London. Javier covered reams of paper so that I would engage with his plight, with his disappointments, with his philosophy and ... his professed love. He imagined that through me there could be another reality that would transform him into someone else. His other self, what he called "*mi otro yo*" would emerge and I would be the agent for this being to come into existence, just as Mary Shelley had given birth to Frankenstein.

> *Querida Estefanía,*
>
> *I am sure you won't tell me everything you think. Women won't divulge their thoughts and I find this very incommoding and equivocal. Life should be less complicated! I want us to discuss everything. You will tell me all your opinions and describe how you see the world.*
>
> *They say that Man is conquered by Woman although the contrary seems to be the case. If I see coldness or disinterest, I leave the field free and I retire. I don't belong to that school of thought that says he that follows her; wins her. In a word, I don't know how to conquer. Maybe this is pride or dignity or whatever you call it. The being that is too sincere, like me, has another defect as well, because I dedicate myself unconditionally and the arrows with which I fight are straight ones.*
>
> *Therefore please believe me when I say that I really like you. If I suspected any of the things I said would "break" our good harmony, I wouldn't tell you anything. A man who wants his love for himself alone – which is a very Arab sentiment – should not be able to possess a woman and demand that she sacrifices her liberty, which is one of the best conditions in life, don't you think?*
>
> *I want to be fair and uncomplicated.*
>
> *For two people to be "almost completely happy" they must be open and there should be no secrets between them. If this doesn't come about from the woman naturally, we men shouldn't "force" intimate thoughts. We should leave her for another.*

Javier had theories about everything, especially about how a woman should be. I hardly thought of myself as a woman. I was only a little older than my charges, but Javier did not take that into account. He wanted me to tell him what I thought, but I didn't know what I thought. I did not believe that "man was conquered by woman" or anything of the kind. I couldn't make out what it might mean for a man to "possess" a woman. I had never known a woman possessed by a man. Mostly the women I knew were left to their own devices. They brought children into the world and cared for them as best they could. They were weighed down by their parental responsibility from which there was no escape.

Javier explained that possession of a woman was an Arab trait, nothing to do with him, but nevertheless in the "*aire*" of Jerez de la Frontera, where people had come to know these ideas because Spaniard and Moor had lived together for many centuries.

I thought possession had something to do with modesty, and was the reason we had to cover our arms. I did wonder why arms were considered to be so tantalising. I knew legs were a problem and should be covered up, but arms? I supposed that if you belonged to one man then another man should not see your arms or your legs – the reason why women in Andalusia had to sit with other women, like we did in the Palacio Garvey. Or like in the old days, when women were only able to look out onto the street from behind big, barred, boxed windows. It might also be the reason why there were no gardens, only interior patios, and not many of them, so that people lived indoors with only an airing in the *Plaza* at the evening *paseo* when the sun went down.

We had modesty in Ireland too. We girls even dressed and undressed without ever taking all our clothes off at the same time. Even if we were by ourselves, we perfected the wriggle required to divest ourselves of clothes under clothes. The nuns told us that we must avoid being "an occasion of sin". They gave us to understand that a man had no self-control and any glimpse of female flesh could drive a man into a frenzy of lust. They said it would be the girl's fault if ever this occurred.

But really women in Ireland didn't pay that much attention to what men said. Men didn't have the same right to put women in their place, which seemed to be the case in Spain. I thought General Franco probably gave men permission to do so because the army was so important and all the men had to do the *mili* and they were all in uniform, which clearly made them feel important.

I didn't bother to tell Javier all of this. He never talked about the *mili* and certainly didn't seem the type to be driven to a fit of lust despite his declarations of love. He was always correct and polite and never spoke of love when we met, just poured it all out in the letters. One thing I did know was that "liberty" was a difficult state to achieve – both for a girl like myself from a genteel but poor Dublin family, or a man of scant material means, such as Javier. Both gentility and poverty were the reasons why I was locked up in this house with a lot of other women, who were very unlike the way I was.

On the whole I wished that Javier would write letters of a simpler kind and not send me missives like this one:

Querida Estefanía,

I hope you understand me. Some time ago I discovered that "to triumph in life" is to be happy but nothing more, if one can be happy without aspirations. I aspired to "a lot" some years ago and I know that complete happiness is possible but not lasting. Do you understand that well?

You think that I chase the impossible. The fact that I want to leave here is because outside I can experience my other me. By working of course. I must work and create myself. Each one must follow the route of his own personality. It's difficult to find the way. Even God doesn't propose to judge a man until the end of his days but.... we must try to "believe" that we understand ourselves.

I believe that I will be more or less happy in the cradle of the world. In some ways I'm very Spanish in the way I can be inspired by a woman for example. This is romanticising. But one has to be practical, though this is "forced". I have to try to control my feelings so as not to seem ridiculous. What I am saying is I need to write down on paper my most intimate secrets – my thoughts.

I would like to feel one step further on in the human chain and leave behind everything I've been up to now. The roots of happiness lie in constancy and work, all this, my "other" personality tells me. I wouldn't mind working to the last, so that I could kill all shades of ridiculous vanity in myself and normalise my pretentions to be "someone important". I need to quench my "inner fire".

I don't think this is giving in but an effort to find the real path of existence and leave dreams to one side...

I hope that what I want to say to you about myself is fully understood without losing a pinch of exactitude.

As the good friends we are, you can presume to know me "almost completely". Your observation will lead you to know how I am.

All this I tell you, without reserve.

Do you think that people should talk about themselves without reserve? I think these profundities have made matters very complicated, haven't they? Well, those are my thoughts. What do you say? Javier

Sometimes Javier showed that he understood there was little point in bombarding me with such weighty matters. I could not respond – I was only a girl, after all. So when he had finished writing his deep thoughts on the subject of "men" and "women" and without receiving an enthusiastic response from me, he retired gracefully… *con gracia*. He made no further attempts to involve me in his odd world. He let me off the hook. He was, after all, a *torero* and understood such subtleties, as he explained: how he would tease and tempt the bull with his cape and then retreat, walking away before the final onslaught. He assured me there would be no such onslaught with regard to me, as I was not a bull but a girl he was wooing. I found his whole approach mystifying.

I am aware that in these pages there is a lot of philosophy, and philosophy unless it is superlative, is tiring. When time passes and we go our way in our worlds, you can remember a little that a good friend of yours gave you Spanish lessons, by correspondence, and you learnt something.

Well there you are, four little quartos yesterday and three today, that's too much for a girl that hasn't even hurt me!

I would be very happy for you if you found yourself and you were happy ever after. Regarding that thing of being happy, I advise you never to fall in love, or, at least, wait for a few years. When you are older you will know that the love you feel – or believe you feel

– is more profound. By then you will be able to think for yourself. You will triumph because you are worth your weight in gold and above all because you have "interior beauty".
Your good friend,
Javier

Chapter Sixteen

In Jerez we bathed every day and showered with the handheld fitment over the bath. We spent a great deal of time caring for our hair.

I was used to washing my hair at most once a week, over a basin, with the stopper trapping used water for reuse, rinsing with the same kettle full of hot water and a cup for scooping it up and over again, and finishing with a last cup of cold water for a clean rinse at the end. A showerhead was a new and welcome instrument for me, as hair care occupied so much of the day. After shampooing, the *niñas* always gave their hair a final rinse with vinegar. Then they sat up on the *azotea* to let the sun do its work and produce copper highlights. They also brushed each other's hair vigorously every night before going to bed. I bought a natural camomile product – *manzanilla* – which bleached my hair blonde without resorting to hydrogen peroxide, the chemical with which Pilar had had so much success in Dublin. She had bleached a cascade of hair to fall over one eye when she looked down. But her hair was of a more luxurious type than mine. Spanish hair was thick, glossy and marvellous in its abundance and could easily support a chemical bath from time to time. My hair however was thin as a spider's web and tawny in colour. Neither was there much of it by comparison. Ma had views as to its care. 'Don't wash it too often, as you will remove the natural oils,' she said. She didn't approve of a fringe either. 'Pull your hair back from the face and let me see your lovely high forehead,' she would say. She did not approve of glamour, with procedures to peroxide hair or paint nails, which were barely tolerated in Ireland. You would have to be "continental" like Pilar to get away with it. But any sign of greasy hair in Spain was unacceptable and showed a slovenly degree of neglect. Only a very slipshod person would be found in such a state.

As with sherry, soaps had a long pedigree of excellence in Spain. They were rated according to the quantity of suds produced as well as by their perfume. Dolores favoured the deliciously scented Heno de Pravia green soap made with olive oil. It came in a plain yellow wrap. She said it was "economical" and "respected the skin", and, in addition to performing the usual functions of cleaning, this soap hydrated, polished and perfumed: *hydratar, reafirmar, perfumar,* as it said on the packet.

La Maja, founded in 1926, was a favourite soap with a famous picture on the luxurious black tissue paper packet: a Sevillana dressed in red, with a long black lace mantilla falling from the tall comb on her head, to drape over one arm. She leaned back with a toe pointed forward and carried an enormous open fan. Reputedly made of roses, jasmine and moss, the soap lathered up well and exuded a distinctive perfume.

The best and most luxurious soap of all was a black soap, the *Magno Classico de la Toja,* which came in a matching black box. It had an unmistakable fragrance, which lingered all day and permeated the tower of white towels in the bathroom. These came in all sizes and included those used to stuff our knickers when the time came for each of us *niñas mayores* to mop up our scant monthly bleeding; the curse of young girls. This was a secret never mentioned between us, although readily discussed by the occupants of the *azotea*. We doused ourselves with *Agua de Colonia* in a variety of flower essences: orange blossom, jasmine and crisp *vetiver* to cover up the acrid smell of our primitive sanitary towels. Soiled towels were removed to the laundry instantly.

As well as my new cleanliness of body with daily showers in Spain (as opposed to only occasional baths at home, except in summer when we were clean from the sea), I got used to the pure delight of fresh linen. My clothes were whisked away to the laundry before I had hardly worn them and Pepa changed our sheets every other day. There was no limit to laundering. Sheets were bleached to keep them white: hardly necessary given the power of the sun on the roof terrace where they dried. They were also starched to a crisp and ironed by hand. The resulting purity made for perfect comfort and although I was never tired, having so little activity to fill the days, I always longed to get into bed at night between the lengths of rasping, scented material. Cleanliness became an addiction; a luxury I well knew required an extraordinary number of female working hours to maintain.

Chapter Seventeen

No event in my seventeen years of life could have prepared me for the Passion of Christ as celebrated in Sevilla. I found the event disturbing and unsettling. At home, religion was something taken for granted in an everyday kind of way. It was customary to undergo some deprivation during Lent, giving up sweets at least and eating less at mealtimes. Easter was then celebrated as a time of solemn church services. Afterwards we could get back to normal and as the evenings were already becoming lighter we could stay out later.

Of all the days of Holy Week, I had liked Holy Thursday best. The day when despite the purple-shrouded holy images of mourning in the churches, the Altars of Repose in the lady chapels were stacked with daffodils and spring flowers. If I visited seven churches throughout the day, I was encouraged to believe I would gain a plenary indulgence – a remission of all sins committed – either for myself, or for a holy soul in purgatory. This required a long walk, from Dun Laoghaire to Blackrock via Glasthule, and it was usually raining. In each church I said the Sorrowful Mysteries of the Rosary, meditating on the sufferings of Jesus as he underwent his ordeal for my sake. There was a burden of responsibility to do this, particularly if one had a deceased relative, as I had.

As my father was dead, I felt it incumbent upon me to make sure he didn't languish too long in purgatory, so the walk and the prayers had a special meaning. Apart from this dutiful aspect, the walk was worth the effort to see the spring flowers, even if they were stacked around a very ordinary plaster image of the Blessed Virgin.

In Jerez, it was easy to visit at least seven very old churches without straying from the neighbourhood. For a start, there were four churches dedicated to the evangelists Matthew, Mark, Luke and John, as well as the vast San Salvador. There was Saint John of Knights, as well as the Convent of Santo Domingo, which altogether, I calculated as I planned a route, made up the seven. Each one of these had many images to venerate. However it wasn't necessary to visit the churches at all, as everything contained within them was mended, polished up and then taken out on to the street in procession: Christ, the Virgin Mary and the saints, all out and about and on parade.

But despite having many churches, the processions in Jerez were not considered to be as grand as those of Sevilla, so it was arranged for us, the *niñas mayores*, to spend Easter in Doña Mariana's childhood home; the Palacio Solís on the Calle Sierpes.

Everyone wanted to tell me about the spectacle I was soon to witness; from the working women in the kitchen to the Señores Marqueses on the ground floor and everyone in between. They told me how the city prepared for weeks ahead, that there were fifty-nine processions and how each church had a band of people, a *cofradía*, dedicated to the cult of a particular statue, or several statues, usually one Christ and one Virgin.

Excitement built up; great were the expectations. What could there be that took up so much time and attention? Radio Sevilla broadcast every detail and there were endless discussions: how much new velvet would be required to cover the base of a float on which an image would be carried? Would the *Virgen de los Remedios* (who was she?) be wearing her blue or her white? What new jewels had been donated to *La Esperanza de Triana?* (Where was Triana?): an emerald from the Marquesa of Medina Sidonia and pearls from the singer Juanita Reina; so many new people to learn about and so many famous names to remember.

Dolores had a sister in the workshop of the *Hermanos Delgado*, responsible for processional regalia and silver. She said that this year there was a lot to be done, including re-plating the silver candelabra for the float of the Transfiguration of Holy Mary of the Greatest Suffering (*Santísima Maria del Major Dolor y Traspaso*), which had become tarnished beyond polishing. But the helmets of the Praetorian Guard, standing by for the judgement of Christ before Pilate and also attending to the swooning mother of God in the arms of John the Apostle (*la virgen desmayada en brazos de San Juan Evangelista*) were polished to obtain a mirror-like sheen.

The *Macarena,* the most wonderful of all the virgins, would be wearing her coronation mantle from the workshop of *Elena Caro*, where the workers – many of them nuns – embroidered and repaired old lace night and day to be ready in time. Rosaries of gold, pearls, turquoise and coral had to be re-strung for all the Virgins, to make them strong enough to withstand the wear and tear of the processions.

We heard about the petitions: prayers answered and requests denied. There was the miraculous recovery of baby Paco from polio. He was able to leave his iron lung and breathe freely when all hope had been lost. There was the young bullfighter from Triana who had recovered from a goring inflicted at the Feria. He would be amongst the Nazarenes of Jesus the Great Power, el *Gran Poder*, walking barefoot in an act of humility to ask for pardon and remission for all his sins. He would not be recognisable from amongst the Nazarenes because all of their faces would be shrouded by material falling from pointed hoods.

During the Spanish Inquisition, anyone who was unfortunate enough to be judged heretical was forced to wear such a hood with a stiff cone, like a dunce's cap, as seen in the paintings of Fransisco de Goya. Heretics refusing to believe Catholic Articles of Faith were condemned. They were the people that didn't fit in and conform and included Moors and Jews, Javier told me.

* * *

During the civil war, Francisco said on one of his nightly visits, many religious images had been stored away. Otherwise these priceless works of art might have been destroyed.

He said that a civil war was a dreadful thing, when brother turned against brother and blood was copiously shed. Many towns and villages in Spain had been ruined and churches burned to the ground. The reds, he said *"los rojos"* had persecuted the Church and even killed nuns and priests as well as destroying holy images. I couldn't imagine anything more sacrilegious. Killing a priest or a nun was unthinkable! He said the *Macarena* had lost her jewels and her crown and that was why when the war was raging she was seen to be wearing the crown of the Virgin of Sweet Name – *la Virgen de Dulce Nombre*. But it was surprising that the Macarena had been on show at all, given that the Virgin of Bitterness – *Virgen de la Amargura* had been placed in a box for storage. The Señora Marquesa showed me a photo of this virgin of sorrowful countenance looking out of the box in which she was stored. She had a reproachful look, as if lamenting the fighting and enmity of the times.

In another photo, the people saluted the virgin with stiff outstretched right arms. This was an old-fashioned salute from Roman times, the Marquesa said, which wasn't favoured any more. It had only been in fashion for a short time after the war.

Francisco told me we had had a civil war in Ireland too. I couldn't imagine that. It must have been ages ago, as no one there ever mentioned such a thing. We had surely never allowed a priest or a nun to be killed.

* * *

The Palacio Solís in the Calle Sierpes was the ideal place from which to watch the processions make their way along the official route established in 1604. We older *niñas* looked down from the wide terrace, craning our necks over the wall to see the floats pass by along the narrow street below making their way to the high altar of the Cathedral. Later they returned to their neighbourhood churches by different routes.

Starting on Palm Sunday, the *cofradías* set out, each one accompanied by a brass band playing funeral marches. A *cofradía* consisted of hooded Nazarenes in parallel files accompanying the floats containing the images. There was variety in the processions: some Nazarenes dressed as Roman guards, others were standard bearers, their pennants embroidered with the insignia of the virgin they supported. Some carried a tall silver candlestick with a lighted candle. Others buckled under the weight of large wooden crosses.

The processions became more elaborate as the week progressed, building up to the night of Holy Thursday to Good Friday. This was the culmination of the festival and we were part of events. For once we circulated freely amongst the people. It was the first time in my life that I had stayed up all night. We waited at the Confitería Campana in the Plaza Campana – the best vantage point from which to watch the processions criss-cross the city. We drank cups of *chocolate* and ate *churros* – fried batter sprinkled with crunchy sugar.

At midnight we made our way to the Puerta de la Macarena – the Bab el Makrina archway with the church set into the ancient Moorish wall at the edge of the city. The Macarena erupted on to the streets into the chatter of the night in a dazzle of light and a great fanfare. We saw her through a haze of candle smoke to the high-pitched wailing of a Sevillian trumpet. Applause rippled through the crowd for the Queen of Heaven rising up above the people in the district after which she was named, *(la reina de los cielos asomándose en su barrio),* surrounded by fresh gardenias scenting the night air. Fifty pairs of *alpargatas*, as if belonging to a big headless insect, shuffled along under the heavy curtain of the solid-silver float. The *costaleros,* not seeing where they were going, bore the great weight on their shoulders. The commander outside shouted instructions and used the knocker at the side of the float: one knock for lift, two to start her off on her journey around the city, three to stop for a break. The boys raised her up. They shook the float to make her dance. Up and down she bobbed and from side to side.

'*Qué gracia,*' said Blanca, which meant how graceful she was and how charming. But I thought she might mean sanctifying grace, that necessary supernatural ingredient of being a Catholic, which allowed a person to believe in the unbelievable. The *costaleros* swung the virgin around the corner into Sierpes at a determined pace. We followed, drawing ever nearer to the float.

I looked on the face of the Macarena, a single crystal tear on her cheek. The people applauded. They clapped and clapped. Caught up in the illusion, I wanted the Macarena to speak. I addressed the image but silently, unlike the people around me, shouting prayers with cries of admiration. I asked the Macarena to take me home.

Sometimes when the procession stopped at intervals a

voice was raised in the crowd – very softly at first and building up to a *saeta* for the virgin, an arrow of sound: *your face, my God your face, that small brown face, my hope, my star.*

I was transfixed, grief stricken, distraught and homesick, weighed down with a sense of loss I could not fathom. Something had happened that I did not understand. The girls put their arms round me.

'Cheer up!' Fatima said. 'It's fiesta. It's not supposed to be sad.'

'But it is sad.' I said. 'People are dead and that's why it's sad. I can feel that it's sad.'

I think I believed I had seen a real apparition. The Macarena was nothing like the Virgin Mary we prayed to in Ireland, the lifeless, plaster meek-and-mild mother dressed in dowdy blue. The Litany of the Blessed Virgin Mary invoked a hundred titles, all of which I knew, words to reflect every virtue, but none adequate to this occasion: my meeting on the streets of Sevilla with the Virgin Mary, dressed in gold and silver brocades and dark velvets and decked in priceless jewels, with a clear crystal tear on her cheek.

We saw other virgins – again and again: the *Trianera* – Our Lady of Hope, patroness of bullfighters, with eyes downcast. We saw the patroness of gypsies – l*a señora de los gitanos* – gazing heavenwards, accompanied by the best *saeta* singers of Andalusia. We joined the supporters of the Virgin of Bitterness, the *Amargura*.

Then I became aware of the other figure of the night, *Cristo el silencioso,* carried without a sound along the route surrounded by penitents – no trumpets, no singing. I saw *El*

Cachorro – Cristo de la Expiración (Francisco Gijón's carved gypsy image from 1682) crossing the bridge over the river Guadalquivir to Triana, the worker area of the city, at dawn, to the sound of bugles and solemn drums. Christ naked on the cross, the penitent Nazarenes overdressed in black garments with white woollen capes. Then, naked, the gypsy Christ, *El Cristo de los Gitanos,* on the cross, rising up from a bed of deep red carnations and purple irises.

Who will lend me a ladder to ascend the cross and remove the crown of thorns from the Nazarene? The same *saeta* repeated again and again by different voices – from balconies, from doorways along the route for the gypsy Christ with blood on his hands:

El Cristo de los gitanos
siempre con sangre en las manos.
¿Quién me presta una escalera
para subir al madero
para quitarle las espinas
del nazareno?

Then, the most dramatic of all: *el Gran Poder* – battered and badly injured, his purple velvet tunic swaying as he staggered in long strides, bent over under the weight of carrying the cross. His movements controlled by the *costaleros*, themselves bent under the great weight. Red carnations heaped at his feet.

Untie his hands, take his thorns away, cried a voice from the crowd.

The Nazarenes spoke to those they knew in the crowd as they went along, adding to the low buzz of conversation. I heard a woman ask one man how he was feeling.

'Dreadful,' he said, 'I can't breathe in here.'

'Slip away then,' she said, 'I'll get you some coffee.'

Another Nazarene dragged a ball and chain along the road. Another had bleeding feet.

Ragamuffin children kept pace on the Calle Javier de la Vega, running in and out of Nazarene skirts to collect the drippings of candle grease from which to make yellow wax balls.

The Nazarenes doled out sweets, *dulces,* from under their robes. The children begged for cigarettes: '*Dáme tabaco*'.

As dawn broke, the Macarena was at the corner of Calle Cuna la Virgen for the first rays of the sun to fall on her face. By then, I certainly expected a miracle: some supernatural sign. I had quite forgotten that the vision I perceived was only a doll made of carved wood.

The Macarena re-entered her church at ten in the morning through the great doors, the *costaleros* on their knees to manoeuvre her inside. The image was left in the aisle, where the flowers wilted and faded and the candles still spluttered in pools of molten wax. After Holy Week, she would be dressed in her everyday robes and restored to her usual niche above the altar in her designated chapel. Once again, the great treasures of the church had been taken out onto the streets and given new life: gold and silver from the New World, priceless sculpture and precious jewels – all stored away to be kept safe for next year.

On Easter Sunday afternoon we went to San Lorenzo to kiss the hands and feet of *el señor de Sevilla, Jesus, el Gran Poder*. We joined the *besamanos* queue to get close to Christ exalted, dynamic and realistic, carved in 1620 from cedar wood with articulated arms and wrists for a dual purpose: to carry the cross and allow the hands to be kissed.

I remembered the visit to the village in Extremadura and the time when Francisco had had his hands kissed after the inaugural mass of the young priest. He had been in *besamanos* like the *Gran Poder*.

The quality of that Holy Thursday night, the perfumes and the sound of trumpets wailing in my ears stayed with me. For weeks after Semana Santa I heard screaming trumpets in my head – a high-pitched beseeching sound, certainly a prayer more powerful than a Hail Mary. I now knew why the women of Andalusia had no difficulty in finding names when it came to baptising their girls. Thenceforth I knew where Dulce, Remedios, Amargura, Esperanza and Macarena came from.

Chapter Eighteen

Javier continued to amuse me with stories. He instructed me as to the details of local life. Food figured largely in his descriptions. He worried about the effects of different kinds of food on his digestive system. The details of every meal were mulled over in the aftermath.

> *I fell ill on Tuesday. I had a heavy supper the night before, I drank too much wine and smoked like a carriage-man, but I think that what did me the worst damage was a fish soup that cut my digestion. I woke up a few times in the night, feeling hot, then cold, then hot again. Maybe there was a lighted cigarette in the bed and I didn't notice. I was very uncomfortable.*

But soon he returned to his favourite subject: How could he escape from Jerez? And how would I figure in his plans?

> *I am sure that for unquiet temperaments, such as mine for example, going away would be a sedative for anxiety. Staying always in one place is like being in prison. Spain is a prison for poor people.*

All my poor projects, I'd like to experience them with you, but without doubt, this would be a disturbance for you.

When I was young, I dreamt of being a train driver, in the next phase I wanted to be a test pilot. But I'm glad I never became one, as given what planes are like in Spain I would be dead by now. I was saved by not knowing any mathematics. Nowadays I dream of travel, travel, travel. It's so sad being poor!

* * *

I first met Patrick, tutor to the children of the Williams and Humbert family, when he came to mass in the Palacio Garvey. He seemed to be seeking extra approval by attending mass in our house. Quite unnecessary, I thought, especially as there were masses all day long for him to attend in the town churches. An Irish boy who sought to impress by attending mass was depressing. He was a stocky boy with glasses. Despite the heat, he wore a tweed suit: square in shape, square by nature I thought to myself.

Another new arrival was May from Scotland, who had red hair and freckles – colouring bound to stir up curiosity in the population and cause havoc with the street boys. She had taken up a position as a Miss, but with a modest family. Her employer was a doctor, nothing to do with sherry.

I introduced Patrick and May to Javier, so now there was a little group of us: May, Patrick, Javier and myself. Patrick talked to Javier about his future prospects, teasing him a little and introducing a lighter note to our friendship. He took on some of the burden of Javier's desire for escape, although I was the only one in receipt of letters.

> *Regarding my journey, I am thinking of talking to Don Emilio, the owner of Los Cáceres hotel, to see if I can organise an exchange with a hotel in England. I've read – I don't know where – that the population of foreign students looking for work is so great that the most fashionable thing to do is to take fat dogs for a walk, so that they lose weight; very long walks at a fast pace. I figure that, in my case, I would do away with the owner of the dog sooner than walk said little animal. Can you imagine me running along at a gymnastic pace pulling two dogs? What's more with those beasts as companions I'd never ever learn the language. The most suitable would be for me to sit in a café and count how many blondes, redheads, tawny heads or brunettes passed by during the day for the English statistics. They could give me a peseta for each one.*
>
> *Patrick says he will laugh when he sees me in the Savoy Hotel in London and I tell him he must not make me laugh, as they'd kick me out immediately. All these things excite me because I need to know life in other aspects and from other points of view.*

Javier belonged in a town where everybody lived from the wealth of sherry. His contemporaries were idle rich boys that had never had to work. He had nothing in common with them and he couldn't join in, as they hadn't even been to school together. The sherry boys spoke English, even among themselves, as many had been educated in English schools. Javier was out of place. He couldn't settle down. He had tried to be a *torero* to gain respect, but I suspected he wasn't a proper torero. The bulls in the photos he gave me were rather small. They were *novillos:* calves less than three years old and not very dangerous; nothing to be afraid of, unlike the big hefty bulls in the posters plastered everywhere that showed a large beast. Javier's bull only came up to his waist. He was looking down at it from a height in the photos, rather than being at eye level in a more equal relationship.

Javier realised that if he spoke good English he would command respect. Then he would be like his peers. He could learn to trade in sherry, although he showed no interest in sherry and hardly noticed that it was the main purpose of existence in the place where he lived.

* * *

A younger clientele had taken over at Los Cisnes. The local señoritos were still there – where else would they go? But the wood-panelled bar was crowded with a different type of patron: a more desirable kind than my *torero* friend, Javier, and certainly more desirable than the dutiful Patrick. American service men had found their way to Jerez de la Frontera from Rota, about twenty kilometres away on the coast.

This was a revelation. The United States of America, a new world to be discovered, just down the road from Jerez. Just to see these soldiers in their olive-green cotton uniforms signalled glamour. It was a perfect shade, matching perfectly with their khaki shirts and black ties.

My head buzzed with possibilities: movies, music and

romance a mere twenty kilometres away. For someone who had recently travelled from Jerez de la Frontera to Dublin and back again, all on my own, on all kinds of transport, it did not seem beyond my capabilities that sometime, not too far in the future, I would get to Rota and investigate. I discussed the possibilities with May. She agreed that there was much excitement to be had from further exploration.

The smart, gum-chewing boys at the bar were refreshingly healthy. I found them deliciously minty. They were more like me, and more my age. They had a natural ease and they were polite. Not that Francisco and the members of my Jerez family were impolite. They were always gracious and charming. So was Javier gracious and charming and full of fun. It was outside the house *en la calle* that life became difficult and rudeness prevailed. The frenzied *piropo* made a walk down town a misery. No wonder women had to be accompanied all the time. In fact Javier had been offered a job to denounce these boys – a ridiculous job, he wrote:

> *There's another employment I could do, denouncing hooligans that go about annoying "ladies" and for each report one gets a proportion of the fine; but this employment is very idiotic and completely ridiculous. Don't you think so?*

I asked Javier why the boys did this. 'They are hooligans, gypsies,' he said. 'They are allowed to do it because before the war and before General Franco took over, women thought they could be the same as men, that they could do whatever they liked. Can you imagine! Now they have been shown their place – *mujer en casa*. That's the way it is now. If a woman as much as opens her mouth, she will be put in her place. That's the law. A woman must be a mother to her children and a support to her husband. She is not expected to play any part outside or elsewhere. In return she gets respect and protection in the family for her labours – *sus labores* – at home.'

I could only hope that a woman did get respect at home, because I hadn't noticed her getting much respect outside on the streets of Jerez. A woman could hardly go out at all without annoyance of one kind or another.

* * *

Javier had strong views about the servicemen from the American naval base at Rota. He didn't approve of them. He thought them worse than the *golfos* he would be paid to denounce. They were a danger to decent women, he said in one letter. He was extremely put out to learn that our friend May had been on a visit to Rota.

> *I don't know what's happened to May. She seems to have disappeared since she went to Rota with the Americans. I know some Americans at the Rota base, and in general, I don't like them at all. They emanate a certain atmosphere, their speech, their dollars. What's more, although there are exceptions, they are very vulgar, muy golfos, and they are stupid. Do you think they have kidnapped her? I am glad you didn't go with her. I wouldn't have liked that. I don't want you seeing those people. You are too good for them.*

Javier was like my brother. They both displayed the same intolerance and snobbery towards boys I might get to know. I would make up my own mind I thought, when it came to deciding who was a "suitable" companion for me. I definitely liked the look of the Americans. They didn't speak Spanish but seemed to manage their dealings locally nevertheless. I watched and noted every nuance of behaviour, but had to be content with only a brief exchange of civilities. Patrick made sure they kept their distance while we drank our *copas* at Los Cisnes.

I asked Francisco about the Americans when he came to wish us *niñas* a good night. He said that General Franco had invited the Americans to Spain to make sure that communists from Russia – also called *rojos* – would never be able to land with their submarines in Spain, as they had nearly done when the Spanish *rojos* were in charge. So the Naval Base at Rota near Cadiz, had been established in 1953 to guard the coast. Together America and Spain would watch out for the whole Mediterranean region. Spain had had enough trouble with communists, both within and without its borders. They had even had a cruel civil war to get rid of them, in which more than a million people died.

'Did people in Jerez die too?' I asked.

'Yes, but we don't talk about that as people might get upset. We don't know if any of their relatives died. It is better to let sleeping dogs lie.'

'What did the *rojos* want?' I asked. 'What were they fighting for?'

'Well, they were against the Catholic Church for a start,'

he said. 'And they didn't believe in private property or in the wealth of the church. That's why they burnt houses and destroyed churches and set fire to any treasures that hadn't been hidden.'

'What happened to all the *rojos?*' I asked him.

'They lost the war,' he said. 'General Franco banned them and they went away.'

'Where did they go?' I asked.

'Who knows, different places. They lost the war, that's all.'

I asked Francisco whether he liked General Franco. Everybody seemed very taken with him. His picture was everywhere, in cafes, bars and government offices and people said "*Franco, Franco, Franco"* in a kind of chant and sometimes stood to attention at the same time. Nobody cheered Eamon de Valera, our Irish president, in the same way. I used to see him on my way to school in Blackrock, as our paths crossed when he was driven to morning mass. He was blind at the end of his life and very religious, forever saying the rosary in the back of his chauffeur-driven car. I wondered why de Valera didn't organise a special dispensation from the Vatican for a mass to be said at home, like the *señores marqueses*.

Franco and de Valera were good friends, Francisco said, as they were both firm Catholics. In fact de Valera was partly Spanish on his father's side, he told me, although the family came from the island of Cuba in the Caribbean, only coming from Spain far back in history.

In answer to my question about whether he liked Franco, Francisco said:

'Actually, we are monarchists. We have always supported the royal family living in exile in Portugal. Our family also lived in exile during the Civil War. One day the royal family will probably return to Spain for good, instead of just coming on hunting trips to the Coto Doñana. General Franco will probably invite them back.'

Chapter Nineteen

My friend Javier – on paper at least – was very attentive. He had different strands to his letter. He worried about his future. He wondered if there was any role for me in his calculations, but also said he had no right to pay court to me, as he had no prospects and anyway I was too young for real romance, although he hinted at one anyway.

> *There are things I shouldn't say, although you deserve to hear them, I think you are very profound and interesting, amongst other things, because you have known the world and its peoples. I would like to know you through and through.*

I mostly ignored his compliments, taking them with a pinch of salt. He said he wanted to know me "through and through", which sounded ominous. But when I met up with him, he was as meek and mild as a lamb. He was never aggressive or pushy – quite different from his letters, in which he exaggerated his feelings. He was happy when I gave him little gifts: a packet of foreign cigarettes or some picture postcards I had brought back from Dublin to give as souvenirs.

> *Querida Estefanía:*
>
> *Now I am smoking one of the cigarettes you gave me and they taste differently from all others. Perhaps it's because I'm reminded of you and I think I have you by my side.*
>
> *Last night I dreamt of the "white whale"; it turned out that it appeared with terrible horns and I started to fight it on top of the water as if it was a gigantic bull creating a great wave all around it. Afterwards, (I don't know how I got out of that) I found myself on terra firma; very green and with exuberant vegetation, it must have been Ireland. It's lovely there! I ended up wandering around a great grey mountain and I woke up suddenly; I had given myself a blow, on my head, with the bedside table. It was a very ordinary dream because you didn't appear anywhere, but nevertheless I thought of you as soon as I woke up and that's the interesting thing because after all, dreams are only dreams ("al fin y al cabo, los sueños, sueños son").*
>
> *Yesterday, Sunday, I was all day waiting on Estefanía. I wanted to be punctual. And I wanted to push the hours forward so that five o'clock would arrive. I liked the last letter you sent, the one from Saturday and I understand it well – a las mil maravillas – palabra – really!*
>
> *I have never felt so happy as being with you. I have always liked my Spanish girls better than foreign girls. But you, I wouldn't change you for anyone in the world. You are, for me, the only person that I would be capable of loving with all my strength. I don't know why this is. Don't ask me, because I can't answer. It's like I always knew you, for years.*

Javier was corny. He knew nothing of other places. I didn't like him harping on about the greenness of Ireland, even in a dream or a letter. It was such a boring description. So annoying! But his bullfighting stories amused me and I thought the white whale a terrific image. I liked the comparison of its fierceness with that of the bull. In fact, I loved all Javier's bullfighting stories. He would tell me about his tussles with the beast. Whether these stories were made up or real, I did not know. It was the same with his dreams, seldom based in reality. I didn't dream myself, or if I did I never remembered in the morning. I had had frightening dreams after my father died and then I stopped dreaming.

I only dreamed awake, standing by my bed. I imagined bad spirits – the banshee and evil devils that had taken him away. They were hiding out in the wardrobe, under the table or always in the shadows. Sometimes I turned on the light and perceived, quite clearly, a little face at the heart of the bare bulb, laughing and chortling. I would dive into my bed and hide under the blankets, topped up with coats when it was very cold. These were imbued with the bodily smells of family members, including my dead father. His coat was amongst them so I was comforted. Over time, this panic of the night receded to leave me forever dreamless. In Spain there were fewer shadows where somebody with magic powers could reside. At least, there were no bad Irish spirits that took people away without explanation.

* * *

Javier had vivid dreams and dreams were important in the stories of Spain; "Life is but a dream," they said *(La Vida es Sueño)*. Javier fought whales and bulls in his dreams. He sometimes acted out his encounters with the bull in the ring when we met, rehearsing every move. In the same way, my brother Paul – being a student of Spanish literature – often pretended to be Don Quixote de la Mancha, the knight who lived a life of delusion or illusion. (A saying in Spanish: *Que ilusion*! meant that something would be wonderful and exciting).

Paul was skinny enough to relish the role. He was especially fond of tilting at imaginary windmills with a long pole as his weapon, just as Javier fought imaginary bulls using a chair for a prop. A skinny horse was always a Rocinante in our circles; a short fat man was a Sancho Panza, and a lovely girl a Dulcinea.

Paul imagined all Spanish girls to be noble and he made each one be a Dulcinea. (I imagine that he even thought that Pilar, who I had introduced him to in Dublin, was from Toboso although she was patently another type of woman altogether, and uninterested in his love of Don Quixote). In this Paul resembled Miguel de Cervantes. He pursued unreasonable romantic goals and suffered a rude awakening if he came across the reality of some women, that on close acquaintance, turned out to be more like the women of the *azotea* of the Palacio Garvey, prone to fits of *carcajadas* when it came to discussion of the opposite sex. As my older brother of pure motives, I did my best to shield him, and I attempted to be as good as possible in his presence. I dreaded the thought that he would think less of me if I failed to live up to his impossible standards. I never told him about my boyfriend Michael, nor could I let on to be interested, say, in the American soldiers at Rota. He imagined that my sole purpose in life was to be as he wished me to be – his creation. He gave me books so as to fill my mind with stories he chose.

But one didn't have to be asleep or mad like Don Quixote to dream. Although I no longer dreamt asleep, daydreaming was a major pastime.

Like Javier, I conjured up romantic legends in which I played a heroic part and where I was the centre of my own drama. My cloistered existence in the Palacio Garvey served to reinforce this tendency. When Javier wrote to me of his dreams, I didn't know then that he was quoting from the work of the 17th century Spanish playwright, Calderón de la Barca:

"Que es la vida? Un frenesí.
Que es la vida? Una ilusión, una sombra, una ficción
Y el mayor bien es pequeño: que toda la vida es sueño
Y los sueños, sueños son."

What is life? A frenzy.
What is life? An illusion, a fiction
And the greatest good is paltry:
for life is a dream and dreams are only dreams.

Chapter Twenty

Paul planned a visit to Jerez to see how I was getting on. He was passing through on his way to meet one of his girl friends from college. I thought his girlfriends were quite peculiar people, not that I got to know any of them because they were so much older than I was – the same age as Pilar and Javier. They were bookish women with no glamour about them. None of them was interested in engaging with me. Nuala, the latest one, was an Irish speaker – of all things. She wore glasses and flat sandals all the year round with the addition of thick socks in winter. I was glad that Paul was coming alone. I would hate to be associated with Nuala, who was bound to attract unfavourable comment in Jerez. I counted the days until his arrival. I craved the presence of someone familiar, someone who knew who I was and where I was from. Paul would be an ally in my struggles, a person from my other "real" world. But I was nervous that the web of deceit in which I was embroiled, created through no fault of my own, would backfire. In the whole matter of Pilar's defection, I felt myself to be the innocent victim, but I was in no position to defend myself.

Paul was the scholar of our family. He had been to school at Belvedere College where he won the James Joyce prize for his stories. He was a graduate in Spanish of Trinity College and aspired to being a writer. He worked in London for Courier arts magazine. He had moved away from Dublin and I thought that by now he was more English than Irish in his ways. English, Irish, I didn't have a clear idea of the difference. History though, seemed to have a lot to do with it. Different things had happened to the peoples of the two islands; including wars, never discussed in Ireland. The nuns at school always said that England put Ireland down and belittled us. The English wanted to rule the island of Ireland and steal the crops. But, they said, we were independent with our own language (which I didn't speak) and religion (Catholic) and we had to be true to our own values and not bother about what happened over the water, where people cared more for the Royal Family than for God. Ireland was a republic, they said, self-contained and self-sufficient. That was why Ireland had not fought in any world war.

But our family was half English, and Ma said that the nuns were too simple to understand the world and that they made things up and invented stories and that wasn't history at all and what was more, Irish soldiers had fought in the Great War, including my own father.

'Don't believe all that rubbish about the Fenians – warrior chiefs climbing through keyholes indeed! Don't listen to those silly women,' she said.

I wondered if I would ever find out what had happened in Ireland and especially in Dublin. There were so many questions surrounding historical events – matters one wasn't supposed to mention. Perhaps the nuns were lying about fighting in O'Connell Street and fighting at the Post Office and about executions of Irish heroes? Martyrs, they were, the nuns said. It was because of them that I couldn't mention my own father, also a fighter, but not of the right kind, although he had joined an Irish regiment when he went to war in Flanders. The effect of this division of fighters into two groups had far reaching consequences in my life and even affected my education, because as well as the disrespect shown towards my teachers, in our household the ancient Irish language my classmates struggled to learn was always referred to scornfully as "mahogany gas-pipes". Anybody who actually spoke this language was called a "gombeen", to be scornfully dismissed by Ma as belonging to a class of person with a small shop-keeper disposition and a petty, small-minded nature.

'Irish is a dreadful language,' she said, 'all hacking and spitting. Don't bother with it…and the way the mouth is contorted to produce the words.'

But my teachers were not stupid, neither were they simple. They just preferred to speak Irish and they were very religious. They also really believed the stories they told us, or most of them anyway, you could tell that they were sincere.

Chapter Twenty-One

Eventually the day came when my brother arrived in Jerez de la Frontera. He stayed in a *pensión de tercera categoría* nearby. He came to see me in the afternoons and we went for walks together at the hour of the *paseo*. He was invited to meet the *personas mayores* in the Palacio Garvey. He made a very good impression with his fluent Spanish. He was also correctly dressed, according to local ideas of how a gentleman should look, in an Irish tweed suit, a shirt with detachable collar and his Trinity College tie (black with diagonal red, green and white stripes). I was proud that my employers would see that I came from a good family of educated decent people, as not only was Paul extremely well versed in Irish literature but Spanish literature as well.

The señores invited Paul to dinner in the grown-up dining room. He regaled them at table with his knowledge of the Spanish Golden Age, discussing Cervantes. He said that the personage he liked most out of all literature, in any language, from any country, was the knight Don Quijote de La Mancha. While this took place, I remained with the *niñas* as usual in the apartment on the second floor. I wished I had been invited to join in as what I liked best of all when at home was hearing Paul discourse at table with great enthusiasm about the work of writers he knew and loved. Of course it would not have been possible for me to join the adults for the repast, even if my brother was their guest, as not even Blanca and Fatima, their very own daughters, were allowed to eat with their parents in the *comedor* of the *personas mayores*, or only on very special occasions.

In one way I was hoping Paul would meet my friends Patrick, May, as well as Javier. But Paul expressed disapproval of me going to Los Cisnes, saying I was too young to go to a bar. I knew they would all be gathered, waiting to see him. I had announced his visit in advance with some excitement. But on reflection I didn't know whether I really did want Paul to meet them, as he had such a superior air about him. He might not be what they were expecting. I was full of doubt, caught between all parties: my friends, the Spanish family and my brother. Perhaps it would be better not to mix them up, better to keep them separate. Also, Paul seemed very different in Spain, somehow out of place and I would be saying too much about myself by introducing my brother to those I knew. It was fine at the Palacio where he was at his best. But I didn't want him to be seen by everybody.

Instead of going to Los Cisnes I went with him to the Moderna Pastelería. I watched as he stood at the counter conversing with the owners. He was delighted to be using his Trinity College Spanish. They seemed to like him and asked about his travels, using the respectful "*usted*" form of address. They congratulated me on having a brother who was a real *caballero* and asked Paul why he didn't come and live in Spain. Paul explained that he worked in London and lived in a flat on the Tottenham Court Road. I recalled the night I had spent with him there on my way to Spain. How he had boiled me an egg, craning his neck out of the window to time the three and a half minutes by the pub clock down the road. That is what bachelors were like, I thought, they could do as they pleased and didn't even need a clock or a watch to divide up the day, but only had to look out of the window whenever they needed to see the time.

Paul's visit lasted for three days. Again, I had mixed feelings about him leaving. I was his little sister and looked up to him but now I felt the gap between us was closing. I too was a traveller and a Spanish speaker, although I hadn't been to Trinity College. Not yet, at any rate. Maybe one day people would look up to me for the very same reason that people looked up to him. Perhaps Paul wouldn't like that, if he ever became aware of that happening.

I would never know what he would have said to my friends. I didn't think he would have been kind to Javier. He would have been annoyed about the letters and maybe thought that Javier was taking liberties by unburdening himself. Maybe he would be jealous that someone else was sending me letters – another pile mounting up beside all those I received from him.

* * *

All too soon he came to find me to say a formal goodbye in our apartment, accompanied by Doña Mariana. Paul said he was glad to see me so well set up and thanked her for looking after me. But in the final moments of his leave-taking all was lost.

'I do hope your mother is not suffering too greatly?' said Doña Mariana.

'No. She is no worse than usual,' said Paul.

'But what about her lung cancer?'

'No, not cancer, just chronic lung disease.'

Mariana looked me up and down and pursed her lips. Nothing more was said and Paul bade farewell to all of us *niñas*, and departed.

Chapter Twenty Two

Doña Mariana arranged for me to go on a weekend retreat where she hoped I would meet other young people. Although she didn't mention the matter regarding Ma's illness directly, she obviously thought a good confession and an Act of Contrition would be in order and that I would sort myself out and return to the Palacio in a better frame of mind. I now had a black mark against me. I was not to be trusted any more, even though I was relieved I didn't have to keep up with the pretence that Ma was dying.

The retreat was held outside Jerez in a *Cortijo*, a long low building within a whitewashed walled garden. I shared a room with a girl of about my own age called Marie-Paz Gonzalez. Marie-Paz was from Madrid. She was visiting Andalusia and had been sent on this retreat for much the same reasons as I had – to meet other girls. She was staying with an aunt and knew no one in the area.

The *Cortijo* was not a religious establishment as such, but a private country house. Set in extensive grounds with outbuildings, it was curtained from the outside world by a veil of dark poplar trees. Concha, a middle-aged woman with shiny grey hair, was the prominent member of the gathering. She dressed in a tartan kilt with a matching stole worn over the shoulder of her pristine white blouse. The other women were passive by comparison, content to smile and converse quietly about their needlework while Concha gave orders. Maidservants, trim in starched uniforms, provided meals.

I had hoped to enjoy the weekend but soon realized that, apart from Marie-Paz, there were few kindred spirits among the dozen or so dumpy girls present.

They were not charming girls like those of our Palacio Garvey, but ordinary country girls on their best behaviour. Most of the day was spent in "meditation" and "reflection". As I already spent a great deal of my time in meditation and reflection, having nothing better to do, this was unappealing.

'You see we are just ordinary people,' said Concha, 'nevertheless we dedicate our lives to God. We have a Plan of Life and believe anyone can be holy. You don't have to join a religious order to be a saint. Any one of you girls can be as saintly as we are.'

As well as her other self-imposed duties, Concha provided evening entertainment. She sang *Sevillanas*, which she accompanied on her guitar. In fact Doña Mariana, and any one of her children, was far more adept when it came to dancing and singing *Sevillanas*. Neither did they hold back when it came to *palmadas*, whereas Concha considered hand clapping and even castanets to be vulgar.

Marie-Paz said we were the guests of the Opus Dei, a new kind of order for the Catholic Church. It was run by wealthy lay-people like Concha, who would open their houses to promote religious activities and in so doing they might become a modern kind of saint, as everything they did – even singing out of tune while strumming on a guitar – was for the Greater Glory of God. They had loads of money, she said, and that was why it was unlikely that any of us could join, if indeed we ever wanted to, which we decided we didn't. In fact we couldn't imagine why we had been invited to this retreat, as the organisers had nothing whatsoever to gain from our presence.

A young priest attended on one of the days to give spiritual guidance and to hear our confessions. I thought I would detain him with my worries regarding the "Resurrection of the Body" and how I couldn't see how this was possible. I thought selecting this subject for discussion would be a fruitful line of theological enquiry, rather than going through the usual confessional rigmarole of sins: pride, lies, disobedience and impure thoughts. I didn't have any impure thoughts, or hadn't had any until ideas were put into my head by the bawdy gaggle on the *azotea*. Certainly I would not disclose any longings I felt for love and affection. Confession was never about love and affection or human need for comfort; it was only ever a recitation of day-to-day trivialities.

The priest and I sat face to face in the salon to formally converse. I thought I would give him a chance to prove himself and engage in a proper conversation, but he was no better than his Irish counterparts when it came to religious debate. He was impatient and lacked enthusiasm.

'I expect you'll understand when you grow up,' he said in

an off-hand way, 'in the meantime don't worry about it. Just make your confession in the normal manner.'

I remembered what Ma had told me, for not only did she disparage my teachers at the convent, but she also had scant respect for priests. 'Priests are just men,' she always said, even though I had two priest uncles, one from either side of the family, as well as two great aunts who were nuns. My uncle Gerald was a well-known Dominican. Ma had had a life-long friendship with a priest, Father Henry Tristram, dating from when she lived in Birmingham as a young woman and attended the Brompton Oratory. He wrote to her throughout his life, the envelopes arriving on our doorstep as regular as clockwork and she would add them to the pile she guarded in the roll-top desk. He even left her a legacy upon his death. The solicitor's letter said: "For Stephanie's education". But Ma said it was a present for *her*, only being a priest he couldn't say that. Father Henry was an "expert" on Cardinal Newman, Ma said, and his ideas were ours. That was the kind of Catholics we were: nothing to do with the Irish kind. Cardinal Newman, a former Protestant, wanted each person to take responsibility for his or her self, and not be consulting the clergy at every step to find out how to behave.

Ma had been brought up in England. Her parents had avoided a convent education for their daughters, saying that nuns didn't know how to educate girls. Given the fact that she had been safeguarded from the nuns in her own girlhood, I thought she could have spared her own daughter that fate which had had disastrous consequences, as here I was adrift in the world with only a rudimentary education and my wits to see me through.

Ma wasn't much of a Catholic despite Cardinal Newman. She never went to mass, saying that all that standing up and sitting down in a closed environment smelling of incense made her feel faint. I covered up for her and lied when the nuns interrogated me as to her attendance. 'She goes to the very early masses,' I said, although Ma was always in her dressing gown until noon.

* * *

I had never met anyone like Marie-Paz. She was different. For a young girl of eighteen, she seemed to know everything. She belonged to a youth movement and attended meetings. As we walked around the grounds of the Cortijo, she instructed me as to her participation in the *Falange* – pronounced *fal – an – kay*. The members wore blue uniforms, she said, with little blue hats like those worn by Air Force pilots. Her eyes gleamed as she explained that there were lots of activities and how they went camping in the Guadarrama Mountains outside Madrid.

'Is it like the Girl Guides?' I asked, because I had been in the Brownies and Girl Guides in Ireland, and knew that these were international youth organisations founded by Lord Baden Powell. His great house, Powerscourt, set in a wonderful park, was our favourite picnic place in County Wicklow.

I recited the Girl Guide motto in English for her to take note:

'I promise to do my best, to do my duty to God and my country, to help other people every day, especially those at home.'

'Yes, it is a bit like Guides,' she said. 'But the *Falange* is a Spanish organisation founded by José Antonio Primo de Rivera. It's not international. We only care about Spain. Spain is a very Catholic country. Other countries don't care about us and we don't care about other countries.'

Any Spaniard could join the Falange as long as they hated *rojos* enough, because Jose Antonio had been shot in the war by *rojos,* Marie-Paz said. It was about being loyal to Spain, and General Franco. She sang the *Falange* song: Face the Sun. It had a quite different tone about it from Campfire is Burning or Cuckaboro Sits on an Old Gum Tree.

> *Cara al sol con la camisa nueva*
> *que tú bordaste en rojo ayer,*
> *me hallará la muerte si me lleva*
> *y no te vuelvo a ver.*
> *Formaré junto a mis compañeros*
> *que hacen guardia sobre los luceros,*
> *impasible el ademán, y están presentes en nuestro afán.*

> Face towards the sun with the new shirt
> that you embroidered in red yesterday.
> Death will take me if it finds me
> and I never see you again.
> I'll fall in beside my companions
> standing guard in the firmament,
> impassive and upright,
> always present in our struggle.

This song, written by José Antonio, explained how the forces loyal to General Franco had won the war and set the *rojos* to flight. It described how *Falangist* soldiers died without fear if they were to be slain by *rojos*. They were united in heaven with their brothers-in-arms. Even the name of those people "*rojos*" sounded dreadful in Spanish, with the harsh *jota* in the middle. The English word "red" was a bland-sounding name by comparison: And why "red" anyway? The other side, the victors, were "*azules*" Marie-Paz said. They wore blue shirts. Did the reds wear red shirts? I asked. They didn't. Red was communist, red was Russian. So why did the *azul* soldier have a red embroidered shirt?

Whatever else about José Antonio, I thought to myself, he certainly wasn't a very good poet. I didn't share my opinion on the merits of his poetry with Marie-Paz.

'We are green in Ireland' I said. 'We always wear green on Saint Patrick's Day to show we are different from England, where they don't wear any particular colour.'

I explained about the shamrock and St Patrick and how he had banished the snakes from Ireland and now Ireland was the only country with no snakes. Even as I spoke about the snakes I could hear Ma's voice in my head telling me not to be so ridiculous. That was a typical nun's story, mixing up history and legend. On the other hand I had never seen a snake in Ireland, although I had seen plenty in Spain, so maybe there was some truth in it.

I asked Marie-Paz where the *rojos* were now, as I had never met one, but they cropped up again and again although no one wanted to tell me about them – not even Javier.

'They were communists. They lost the war and the Generalísimo took over. Those that didn't go away had to shut up and support Franco if they wanted to stay, otherwise they got into serious trouble and could even be killed for treason; which is the sin of betraying your country.'

'Are they good or bad people?' I asked. 'They must be bad or why else would they be killed? Maybe they had a reason for betraying their country.'

Although the grounds of the Cortijo felt spooky enough as we paraded around the estate arm in arm, I didn't realise then that we were in a haunted place of bones and that murdered *rojos* lay under our very feet. How could I have guessed such a thing? How was I to know? (Marie-Paz, despite bearing the name "peace", would have been happy to walk on such bones anyway).

'*No te metas en política,*' she said. 'Keep away from politics. You might get into trouble,' and she issued a generous invitation: 'If you ever come to Madrid, I'll take you to a meeting of the *Falange* and you'll see for yourself how our side got rid of communism.'

'I don't suppose I'll ever be allowed go to Madrid,' I said.

She didn't seem pleased that I worked for the sherry people of Jerez; my family owning the Bodega Garvey and being related to all the other bodega families by marriage.

'*Mierda,*' said Marie-Paz, and she said it in a more emphatic way from the way Pepa said it – a *palabrota* muttered when she had to pick up our clothes from the floor while she was cleaning our rooms in the Palacio.

'Those people own everything in Spain. It shouldn't be allowed.'

'They are quite nice people,' I said, 'very Catholic, nicer than the people here in this Cortijo. They are more fun to be with; they have more *gracia*.'

'Being Catholic is one thing, but owning everything is something else,' said Marie-Paz.

Chapter Twenty Three

Despite efforts made by the Spanish family to make my life more interesting, I was heartily sick of my own company, full of energy and bored with the inactivity of day-to-day life in Spain. I wondered if my captivity would ever end and what I would do if it did.

Ma always said that the devil finds work for idle hands to do, but it was my idle mind that Satan was soon to engage as I conceived of a plan to relieve the monotony.

The American Navy at the Port of Rota was some twenty miles away, where ships from America stopped over. Young American sailors were stationed there. Some lived with their young families and it was as if they had never left home.

I decided that somehow I would get to Rota to see what it was like. I would put my mind to it and make a plan. I mulled over the details in my head. I would have to find an excuse to be away from the Palacio. I would need transport and someone would have to take me there. I didn't know of anyone yet, but something would turn up. My mind played with different possibilities. Would I go in the daytime or by night? I did not intend to be away all night but if I missed the ten o'clock cut-off point, when the great doors closed for the night, I would be unable to re-enter the house and this would leave me on the street where I would be discovered by the *sereno,* with unspeakable consequences. If I attempted to hitch a lift, I might be picked up by the Guardia Civil that patrolled the highway: the instantly recognisable Guardia, wearing their shiny black patent leather hats with an upturned flap at the back; the Guardia feared by all, only ever spoken about with bated breath.

I had to be careful to conceal my interest in the American base from Javier, who was proprietorial in my regard and even at times parental, just as Paul was proprietorial and parental. In Paul's case this was justified by the absence of my father and the age gap between us, so at least he had some right to be interested in my well-being. If it weren't for him I would have no one to look out for me. Javier was another matter. Like Paul, he was much older than I was, but I didn't really know where his interests lay. His letters had become ever more elaborate. He was anxious to go to London. Was this the real motive for his professed love and friendship? As I had already been drawn into Pilar's grand plan to escape from Jerez – never having heard a word from her since she had achieved her ambition – I was mistrustful. I had been roundly compromised having borrowed money from my employers under false pretences. I was still in serious debt. I had also been forced to return to Dublin before the allotted time, with all the emotional upheaval this had entailed. Unaccompanied, I had suffered great indignities in third-class railway carriages, travelling across the length of Spain, France, and a part of England and Wales. I had endured two steerage crossings of the Irish Sea. Given all this hardship and the way I had been treated by so-called "friends" I had learned that I could not trust anyone in Spain, in case they had an ulterior motive. Neither could I rely on any support from home; I couldn't even explain my predicament to Ma. I was too proud to confess my difficulties and kept up appearances that I was coping. Moreover, I had been caught out with the lie that my mother had cancer, when really she had chronic emphysema, which would only have consequences in the long term.

So however much I would like to have offered Javier hope, I was wary of making promises to him, although I did say I would write to my brother again and see if he had any suggestions regarding a working arrangement for him in London, even though my brother had shown no interest in meeting Javier when he came on his visit.

> *I'm glad you will write to your brother in London. I think it's a grand idea. I hope these plans will come to something. It seems that everybody I know gets a job except me. I don't understand it.*
>
> *From now on I promise to be really serious and only think of work – but over there, not here. I would be so happy just to be away. I will see if I can be practical and formal in my dealings. Let's see if in changing my way of being, I will improve my horizons. I would like to owe my happiness to you.*
>
> *My mother told me many times that what would have suited me was to be in the middle of the world without a centavo and then see how I got on. She is right. In that way I would have reacted ages ago and it is more or less what I imagine doing now.*

Will you tell me what you like best about my letters? And what you like least? Don't you know how to answer me?
You are always in my heart! Javier

* * *

One day I went alone to the police station. No one from the Palacio was free to take me there. I was in danger of overshooting the date when I should report, which would result in complications. As usual the impertinent *guardia* looked me up and down when I presented my passport for the three-monthly stamp.

'Still here?' he enquired, directing his phlegm into the *Escupidor*. 'When are you going home? Why do you want to stay here where you don't belong?'

After I had completed the necessary formalities and was making my way back through the streets, it occurred to me to return via the Avenida José Antonio. I could look into Los Cisnes to see what was happening. This might be one of the only opportunities I had to go there alone. I dashed through the front doors and went straight to the pink marbled Ladies Room, where I loitered. It was early evening and a reasonable time of day to be out alone. I tried to think of an excuse to approach the bar. I could see from the vestibule that a couple of American boys were propping up the counter. I thought I could just ask for a glass of water. I approached the bar. The waiter knew me. I told him I was waiting for my friend May.

I didn't think he believed me. He knew I was alone and

he watched me as he polished the glasses. One of the boys at the bar was fair. His hair stood up like a brush. The other was slighter, darker; he could even have been from Spain.

'Well, hi,' said the blonde boy. 'Do you speak English?'

'I do,' I said.

'Well have a drink.'

'I had better not. I'm not supposed to be here. If anyone sees me talking to you, I'll be in deep trouble.'

'Oh come on,' said the blonde boy, 'we are not dangerous at all.'

'I'll have a cup of chocolate,' I said.

The thick, brown, viscous liquid was served at the bar. For the first time I found myself standing there, instead of sitting with my legs tucked decorously under the barrier of a table.

'It's great to speak English to somebody from outside the base,' said the blonde boy, who said his name was Gerry Parker. His friend was called Max. They smoked long, white, minty cigarettes. The clean, sharp smell was pure fresh air compared to the black tobacco smoked by the locals, which I considered to be another dirty Spanish habit (like the use of a spittoon) whereby cigarette papers and tobacco were bought separately at the *quiosco,* and made into a smelly makeshift roll. In fact I knew the two disgusting habits were related; without the tobacco, there would be no need for the spittoon. José, my enemy, was one of the worst offenders. He would leave his post at the *portería* and step out onto the street for a smoke. When anyone important came along, he cupped the fag in his hands behind his back and must have burned himself, although he never let on. The palm of his right hand was yellow, stained with nicotine. Disgusting, I thought, but his little *pitillos* bore no resemblance to the fat, brown *puros* smoked by the *señoritos* in Los Cisnes, or the small cheroots they also favoured. The bar was permeated with the sickly-sweet, pungent smell I had grown accustomed to, although I didn't smoke myself. This mint of the green-packeted cigarettes smoked by Americans hinted of a purer place than Spain.

'Go on,' said Gerry Parker. 'Have something else. Let me get you a nice, sweet sherry, a nice Pedro Jimenez.'

I declined and said I really had to rush. There would be dire consequences, if I were to be caught talking to them. The boys asked if they could see me again. I said I would try to get away from the house and that a Friday evening was probably the best time, when the girls had *Sevillana* dancing lessons.

I finished my cup of chocolate and scuttled back to the Palacio.

José looked me up and down suspiciously.

'Why did you go out alone?' he asked. José was an eternal spy, policing the *portón*. I couldn't imagine how Carmen put up with him, although she didn't much, as they had different timetables without any overlap.

'I had to have my passport stamped.'

'I thought you had already been to report to the police this month?'

'*No es verdad!*' I said self-righteously, as at least in that aspect of my life he was wrong.

* * *

I managed to pass Los Cisnes again two weeks later on the Friday. Gerry Parker was there. I accepted another cup of chocolate. He said he had been looking for me everywhere and he wanted to take me out on a date: my heart's desire, an American date. I said I wanted to see the base at Rota, as I was sure it was just the same as going to America itself. He laughed and said it wasn't really but I could see for myself, as I could go there with him at some time in the future.

He wanted to take me to the fair ground at San Fernando where there was a big Ferris wheel, a *noria,* he said, and when the little cabin in which one sat reached the highest point one could see for miles out over the Puerto de Santa Maria and beyond to Africa. He said there was a shop at the base – the PX – where I could buy American things.

We made elaborate plans for the forthcoming excursion. He said if he didn't see me at Los Cisnes he would leave a note there with the waiter to tell me about arrangements.

Chapter Twenty Four

My life was full of subterfuge. Everyone regarded me with suspicion and even Javier complained that I was trying to avoid him. Like José the porter, he was watching my movements although he hadn't witnessed my encounter with the Americans. I wasn't doing anything different as yet, only having conversations in my own language with the boys at Los Cisnes. I only had an *idea* of taking things further, knowing that I would like to go to Rota and find out about America. The plan I made to go there with Gerry Parker was a shaky one; there would be hitches along the way. I might not even manage to achieve the goal I had set myself. Javier seemed to sense something. His letters were reproachful. He had become a nag, a scold and a bore:

> Querida Estefanía,
> I got your card. I was waiting impatiently. You are getting lazy in my regard. Why don't you like writing to me? I imagine you got my letter on Monday? You say nothing.
> If you can't stay out until 9.30pm, we'll have to see each

other before. I'll wait for you on Saturday – the same place as usual, at seven. Will you come? If you can't, tell our friend Patricio.

Soon, I start work in the bottle factory as assistant to the chemist. My hours of work are from 9 to 1.30 then from 3.30 to 6.30. Saturday afternoon is free.

We'll talk about your life when we sit together for a quiet chat. I've got so much to tell you. I continue thinking – and not dreaming – that we could meet in some better circumstances. I don't know what you think of me: "Ay, how weak he is in life and he has no will power." I do have enough will power to love you. Clearly, not much will is required to live for you. It's enough to love you like I do, without knowing why or when I fell in love with you.

Answer me in English. I don't mind – put the odd word in Spanish, so I won't be left without understanding.

Go on, take up the pen and write to me, right now, a long interminable letter.

In truth, I didn't believe his declarations of love. Since I now had more to think about, I barely scanned the letters and was blasé about receiving them, shoving them in a drawer straightaway because it was a huge effort to have to answer them, even with my little dictionary. I had to summon up every ounce of concentration I possessed. From my point of view, we were engaged in word games more than love games and besides, my romantic ideals now lay elsewhere. His ardour, such as it was as when we actually met he made no reference to the devotion he displayed in his letters, was unrequited. He never made an affectionate move to hold my hand or kiss my cheek, but then we always met in public places. I wondered if I would have liked him better had he tried to kiss me, like Dublin boys did, always trying to touch and feel. Javier was more like one of my girlfriends in that respect.

I was so used to accepting the attentions of those who wrote me letters that I took Javier's dedication to the written word for granted, even though my other correspondent Paul, just like Javier, paid me scant attention when I was actually present in his company.

Because of my preoccupations, I must have had a troubled air about me. Señorita became aware that I was distracted and reported me to Dolores, who told Doña Mariana. My days came under scrutiny. My phone calls and letters were monitored.

The momentum built up and together they decided to act, entering my room when I was detained in the *casa de campo* with the *niñas,* in order to rummage amongst my things. Javier's letters were found and scrutinised, although I afterwards realised they hadn't been read in detail. Had they read them, they would have discovered how blameless my life was, just letters from my brother destined to boost my morale, and those from Javier. Although these strayed into areas of romance, above all they revealed his frustration and desire to escape from Jerez to a place where he would be appreciated. He wrote to me, I thought, not least because he had a gift for writing eloquent Castilian Spanish and had no other outlet for his talent.

I had to write and tell Javier what had happened. He was mortified, outraged to be exposed in such a cruel way.

Andaluz himself, with a keen sense of good manners and acceptable behaviour, he could not believe that my privacy had been violated and our friendship called into question.

My phone calls were also called into question, as it was said that some man: "*algun hombre*", perhaps Javier, was constantly ringing up and making a nuisance of himself.

For me, being interrogated on such trumped-up charges was a serious matter, further emphasising my lack of freedom. This was the second time that the family was sending away a friend of mine. They seemed to conspire to keep me in total isolation.

Javier's written response to the situation, which I showed to Doña Mariana, soon came.

> *My good friend Estefañia,*
>
> *You can be completely sure that since Saturday 17th when I called you because you didn't come to our meeting, I haven't phoned. It must be a mistake. Possibly some other friend of yours called pretending to be me. I don't believe that. Neither do I believe that the Señores, given that they are persons of such high standing, could have read your correspondence. Letters are very personal things and both here and elsewhere it is a grave dereliction to read them – even for one's parents to read one's letters is unthinkable. Apart from the fact that letters are sacred and personal to the two people involved. Where is all this coming from? I don't understand the ridiculous things happening. I don't think there is anything wrong in our being friends and seeing each other only three times a month.*
>
> *I know very well where my duty lies and I have nothing against us not seeing each other ever again. I feel truly bad that*

matters have been interpreted in the wrong way and it hurts me that you have been in trouble through my fault.
   Greetings from your good friend,
   Javier

Although I was not attached to Javier in a romantic way, I was deeply upset at how he had been treated. I could not impose my own values of respect for other people on my situation. It seemed that all comers were to be treated with suspicion. I determined that from that day on, I would pay no attention to the stupid strictures of the household. My blood was up. I was ready to break as many rules as possible.

With regard to Gerry Parker, I had to protect this friendship. This one was full of promise. I wondered what the PX would be like and what I could buy there. Above all, I was not prepared for him to be sent away, dismissed, as in the case of Michael, or even Javier.

The Javier episode blew over in a short time. I think Doña Mariana felt she had made too big a fuss. She didn't refer to the letters again. She must have felt guilty at having broken fundamental privacy rules, especially after reading Javier's letter of reproach written as a response to her searching my room. Cautiously, we resumed our correspondence. Sometimes we even drank Lipton Tea together, although, once, I stood him up at the Moderna Pastelería, being loath to expend the energy required to entertain him.

Chapter Twenty Five

Gerry Parker had left me a note with the friendly barman at Los Cisnes, stating the time and place where he would wait for me. I could not ask for permission to go, nor tell anyone in the Palacio that I had been invited to visit the American base at Rota. However I involved May in my plans so that she would give me an alibi for the outing. I said I would report to her on the evening of the day by eight o'clock at the latest, as I had to be back before the *portón* closed. The girls were in Sevilla with their parents and for once they didn't take me with them. I obtained permission from Dolores to go with May to Cadiz by bus. Having thus covered myself, I went to meet Gerry Parker at the designated place of rendezvous.

I escaped from the house when José's back was turned so I wouldn't be subject to the usual interrogation. I had learnt how to do this when he was busy organising food deliveries to the *azotea* via the service lift, or taking the mail to the first floor. He was never gone for long so I had to be quick.

I met Gerry Parker in a *pastelería* off the beaten track as far away from the house as possible. He wore washed-out blue jeans and a t-shirt. Blue denim jeans – only worn by Americans – were just as noticeable as any uniform in Jerez. He stood out. So did I stand out. In a country of short, dark people, where everyone dressed in dark clothes and according to their means and position in society, it was not possible for us to be as inconspicuous as I would have liked. It was because of his brush haircut, and the fact that we were both blonde and taller than the locals. He was also driving an old convertible car, which also stood out. We had to leave the town behind us without delay or the Guardia would definitely be after us. I got into the back seat and ducked down until we were clear of Jerez.

Chapter Twenty-Six

It took three quarters of an hour to reach the American Naval Base at Rota – a short ride to reach another world – *otro mundo*. Gerry Parker knew the soldiers manning the checkpoint where I showed my passport. 'Welcome to the Gateway of the Mediterranean,' one of them said, and we were admitted without delay, past the barrier to emerge on the other side in a place populated by military personnel dressed in olive green uniforms. Excitement surged: I was Alice tumbling down the rabbit hole or crashing through the looking glass. I was the child emerging from the back of a wardrobe. I was the heroine of my own fairy tale, having real adventures. I was alive! Here was another place I would find out about. Javier was right; I was "profound and interesting". I did know an awful lot of things about the world. I could compare places, one with another and contrast them. I was already very well travelled with a great deal of experience.

Here was a place where low buildings of one storey were built within patches of scrubby gardens: quite different from Jerez houses where ordinary people lived: built all of a piece in rows, with barred box windows, and streets so narrow you could almost touch both sides of the road if you stretched your arms out; and where you could hear everything the neighbours said, or snatches of flamenco singing as echoes of the distinctive Jerezano voices reverberated from the stonework. That is, unless you lived in a *palacio* – as the back of the Palacio where I lived was silent, bleak and dingy with windows facing into dark wells where sunshine was never admitted.

We drove around the complex. I saw warehouses and hangers for aeroplanes. A grey ship was docked at the quay.

'Just on a stopover,' said Gerry Parker. 'The ships come and go.'

Sometimes his superiors allowed him to take visitors on board a docked American battleship for a look around. Maybe next time I came I would be able to visit. In answer to my questions about his work, he said he was mostly on guard duty and there was lots of drilling and exercising and learning how to use weapons.

We parked up and headed for the leisure area (pronounced "leejure"). This was what I had come to see! More and more warehouses with different things going on in each one. Although it was lunchtime (not late Spanish lunchtime), we went for an American breakfast in a cafeteria at the back of one warehouse. We queued for food served from flat steel serving dishes. Gerry Parker had bacon and eggs and a few things I didn't recognise. I had a very mustardy bacon roll with extra tomato ketchup. I hadn't eaten bacon in a long time and always missed my home fry-ups, although this breakfast didn't bear much resemblance to the Irish kind.

Gerry Parker urged me to try a potato cake called a "hash brown". It was vastly inferior to an Irish potato cake, which had melted butter added in with the flour and mash, ending up with a toasted coat from the frying in dripping. But this bacon and potato cake had no taste at all. Not even the bacon. How could bacon have so little taste? We drank weak coffee without much flavour, but at least the milk was familiar and delicious, pasteurised – just like at home – without the skin of Spanish boiled milk.

After breakfast we went to the PX – a vast shopping area. Gerry Parker said I could mooch around and buy any small things I liked. I saw young girls, not much older than I was with babies in pushchairs. I wondered what it would be like to change places with one of them. I could be married with my own baby. I could be married to Gerry Parker. How would that be? Would I feel free then? Would I be able to make my own decisions and stop being weighed down with other people's demands? At least I wouldn't have to earn my own living.

Besides food in unfamiliar packaging, there were clothes at the PX, women's shorts and shirts in horrible colours not to my liking. Anyway nobody wore shorts in Spain so what good would they be outside the base. Imagine if Doña Mariana, Dolores or Pepa all wore shorts – unthinkable!

I was introduced to American chocolate, the Hershey bars that again came off badly when compared to Cadbury's Dairy Milk. There was chewing gum – nothing new there. We had chewing gum in Ireland, and Spain had its own *Chiclet,* with which to exercise the jaws when we weren't cracking *pipas,* and never to be chewed in public.

The make-up section was exciting. I put lipstick and eyeliner as well as eye shadow into my shopping basket, imagining how glamorous I would look with a black line painted over the edge of my eyelid and a turned-up flick at the outer edge to give a slit effect.

I looked at magazines. I didn't think I could take them back to the Palacio, as they would give me away completely if the women decided to search my room again. However, in the end I gave in to temptation and bought a magazine called McCalls and a Women's Home Journal. Both had features providing cleaning tips with suggestions for running a home correctly. There was an Agony Aunt page for girls to discuss their boyfriend problems.

I couldn't pay for the purchases at the checkout myself – *pesetas* were not accepted in this part of America-in-Spain – but Gerry Parker was as good as his word and paid up with surprisingly small, greenback dollars. I immediately faced another dilemma. Should I be accepting this generosity? But I couldn't bear the thought of throwing my purchases away – especially not the make-up.

Neither could I part with the magazines. I would have to smuggle them into the Palacio anyway and keep them under my mattress, hoping that my room would not be searched again. After all, I could always throw the magazines away if they looked like being discovered. Although that would not be easy in a household where rubbish was inspected on the way to the bins.

After shopping, we went to a bar where American servicemen drank beer and called loudly to each other across a room. Gerry Parker's friend, Max joined us and he congratulated me on escaping from Jerez for a day.

We spent a couple of hours listening to American music blaring from the largest and brashest jukebox I had ever seen: all chrome and mirrors and coloured intestines. From time to time a soldier would insert coins into the gaudy box and set the mechanical arm visible within the machine moving across the columns of records, to pick out the numbered selection. As an ardent Radio Luxemburg listener, I was conversant with rock and roll as were all my friends in Dublin. I knew most of the records on the jukebox intimately, except for the latest ones. I was out of touch. I missed pop songs. American music was far too vulgar to be ever heard at the Palacio so never a hint of the new songs came my way.

I discovered that Gerry Parker only liked smoochy music: Nat King Cole and Johnny Mathis. This was disappointing. But as the day progressed, I learned to appreciate the smooth sounds of easy-listening jazz; Johnny Mathis singing dead slow to a tinkly piano:

> "It's not for me to say you love me
> It's not for me to say you'll always care…"

* * *

The fairground was outside the American Base at the port of Rota in San Fernando. The giant wheel could be seen from afar. It had a metal structure with little green painted carriages

– like rocking boats – hanging from the wheel and remaining stable as the wheel went around. The Spanish called this fairground apparatus a *"noria"*, after a large revolving wheel in the countryside for irrigation purposes, that had buckets of water placed at intervals dipping and filling from a river as the wheel turned, before spilling over onto the crops below.

I entered into the little rocking boat with Gerry Parker – a place of privacy suspended in space – keeping steady as the world dipped away. We arranged ourselves opposite each other to distribute the weight, and the little boat rocked softly.

It was true that when we reached the highest point of the wheel we could look out towards Africa over misty blue sea and sky. It was true that one felt dizzy with the motion. But better than the view by far and dizzier than the motion, were the softer-than-butter, sweeter than Pedro Jimenez, American kisses we exchanged. No hurry, no interruptions; the close exploration of features and the contours of a face in time and space suspended.

> "As far as I can see this is heaven,
> and speaking just for me
> it's ours to share.
> Perhaps the glow of love will grow with every passing day…
OR
> we may never meet again, but then
> it's not for me to say…"

* * *

We rushed to get back to Jerez before dark. Gerry Parker dropped me off in an out-of-the way *barrio* of Jerez so the car wouldn't be spotted, but it was after 10 pm and the *paseo* was long over. I thought I recognised the place, but it turned out I didn't. I heard sounds of music coming from a tavern – guitars tuning up. A few clacks of castanets; *zapateo* and then silence, a woman's voice raised in a kind of sob – a moaning lamentation, and it was not even *Semana Santa*. Here I was in the middle of Jerez with the *portón* of the Palacio firmly closed to me and nothing bad was happening. I entered the bar boldly and asked to use the phone. 'Of course *querida*,' said the large woman with huge arms and brown skin and a smile wide enough to show her gold teeth. 'Who do you want to telephone?'

May. I would ring May. I prayed May would be available and that my fall-back plan would work. And it did.

'My son will take you to the Calle José Antonio, *guapa*,' said the bar woman, 'and don't you worry.'

While I waited I accepted a cup of chocolate prepared by the woman with the gold teeth and large hooped earrings. I took in my surroundings. Chairs were arranged in a circle for an old couple and a guitarist playing *bulerías*. Three girls in spotted, long-trained dresses practised their clackety clack chatter of castanets…

I wished I could stay to hear them but the boy was in a hurry to take me to May and return to his dancing.

So there I was walking the streets of Jerez at nearly midnight, with a slim, polite gypsy boy. What further exciting things could happen to me all in one day?

May was as good as her word. She met me in the street and took me to her room. She was able to do this, as her family, being of only reasonable wealth, had neither *portón* nor *portero*.

Chapter Twenty-Seven

I was supposed to have spent the day with May, but I had not said anything about the night. Perhaps I hadn't been missed? The girls were away with their parents in Sevilla so they wouldn't know I wasn't there. I had returned late from Rota but at least I had got back and was safely tucked up in May's bedroom. Nevertheless I was overcome with guilt. I could have reported to Dolores right then and said I was staying the night with my friend. But in my panic I decided on another strategy. I would pretend I had been in the Palacio all the time. I tossed and turned unable to sleep and counted the hours from the chimes of the church bells. I got up when I heard the morning mass bell from Santo Domingo. I borrowed a black mass veil from May and scurried through the streets. Dolores would be along soon, as she really did go to early mass at Santo Domingo. The door was unattended. I thought I would slip through. No such luck! José, ever-present, emerged from the *portería*.

'Where have you been?' he asked. 'It is six o'clock in the morning. You have been out all night.'

'No, I haven't,' I said. 'I was here. I just decided to go to early mass.'

'Lies,' he said. 'Always lies! I will report you to the Señores when they get back from Sevilla. Go to your room and Dolores will find you there.'

I went to my room overcome with shame. Why had I made up such a stupid story? I was the author of my own downfall. If I hadn't been paralysed with guilt, I could have handled the whole situation. I had spent so much time scheming to get to Rota and my adventure had gone off like clockwork and then I had tied myself up in knots for no reason and all for a few kisses – however wonderful these had turned out to be – with an American soldier.

Dolores brought me my meals on a tray: fruit and biscuits and grey milk with *nata*. I was back where I had started just fifteen months after my arrival.

A huge fuss ensued when the family returned from Sevilla. I was summoned to the salon on the first floor for my employers to interrogate me. Dolores stood at the door as if to guard against my escape. Where had I been? Who was ringing me up? They demanded to know. I remained silent, said nothing to defend myself.

I couldn't divulge the details of my adventure. What would they think if they knew I had been on a date with an American? This would be the worst of all possible circumstances they could imagine. They saw my silence as defiance.

A great coldness descended.

I was confined to my room. Blanca and Fatima hardly dared speak to me when I emerged for meals, which seemed to take much longer than usual as we waited at table. Maria and Marianita were unaware of the tension and prattled away as usual. Afterwards I was again confined to my room *"en penitencia"* separated from the *niñas*.

Rebellion set in. I set to work with the make-up I had bought at the PX. I outlined my eyes in deep black and smeared purple eye shadow over the lids. I looked like the chameleon on the bougainvillea of the *casa de campo*, which changed colour to match whichever leaf it was hiding under or turned grey when it retreated to the masonry in the heat of the day. Like mine, its eyes were bulging and sultry, I hardly recognised myself. Perhaps this was *"mi otra yo"* emerging; the other self Javier talked about. My old self was being left behind, that was for sure, another person was taking over. I put on the blue dress with the square neck and bulked it out with the hooped petticoat. Then I sat and waited. I felt fine; I could speak good Spanish, I was glamorous and had been kissed. But my gestures of defiance went unremarked and ignored. Eventually I collapsed into the usual state of apathy, lying on my bed, waiting.

After what seemed like a week had passed, Doña Mariana came to our dining room one lunchtime.

'Go and take off that makeup and cover your arms,' she said. I was wearing the flame sleeveless dress I had fashioned to my own design at the *costurera*, 'then come with me.'

She had booked my plane ticket for the following day. I was to be driven to Sevilla that afternoon.

'You have been deceitful,' she said. 'You have told lies about your mother and made us give you money to go and see her, believing she was gravely ill. You ordered inappropriate sleeveless dresses from the dressmaker – like the one you are wearing at the moment. You have been hanging around the hotel Los Cisnes without a chaperone and you have caused a scandal with various men allowing them to write you letters and ring you up. What is more, when we were away you stayed out all night; God knows what you were doing.'

I said I was with May, but they didn't believe me. It was observed that we hadn't been to Cadiz on the bus and they didn't believe that I had been with her all night, even though when questioned she swore that was the case, which it was. They believed they had evidence to stack against me.

I said the letters were from my brother and Javier, whose only motive was to teach me Spanish, but to no avail. Apart from the omission of my American adventure, everything I said was true, but I could not defend myself. I didn't bother to try. There was no point. I should have told them that no one could live in such an atmosphere of suspicion: that they had even been suspicious of Michael, when he came to see me from Dublin. Anyway, one half of me was glad to be leaving. I would be able to start my life over again.

'Dolores and Pepa will pack your bags and I don't want you to see the girls again,' said Mariana. 'You have been a very bad example.'

Even in the disappointment I felt as to the lack of understanding shown to me, I was devastated by Mariana's coldness and anger. Of all people, she was the one I longed to impress. I had wanted her to like me and maybe consider me as one of her many daughters. Maybe I could be like them, I thought sometimes. I could assume their gaiety and grace and their serious approach to life. But my disgrace had put paid to all such fantasies.

* * *

There was a timid knock on the door of the room where I was waiting. Blanca and Fatima stood outside and whispered goodbye. They said they wouldn't forget me. I was crying. So were they. They held my hands and kissed me on both cheeks. Blanca passed me a card: a holy picture of the *Trianera* in full *Semana Santa* robes, wearing her high silver crown and swathed in lace. It was dedicated in the subjunctive:

"For Stephanie, that she should have a little souvenir of Blanca."

Para Stefani, para que tenga un pequeño recuerdo de Blanca.

Chapter Twenty-Eight

I was back in Dublin before I could process the details of my disgrace. So much had happened since I had been away. The people I had left behind were surprised to see me back home again before time although there was nothing very remarkable in that. I was too proud to say I had been sacked from my position and sent home ignominiously.

In Dublin there were many who left for adventures abroad. And there were those that emigrated for a better life in a wealthy under populated country, such as Canada, Australia or the United States of America. Many returned, settling back into their native place, their adventure becoming a distant recollection. I hoped that wasn't going to be the case with me.

I couldn't imagine what I would find to do next. I was afraid of becoming a burden. But Ma was to ensure that didn't happen. She was unperturbed by my sudden return. 'Cheer up,' she told me, 'it's not the end of the world.' She was only a bit rattled when a Solicitor's Letter came from Rita's mother, demanding the repayment of the £10 debt I had incurred. She paid up without demur however, accepting that the money had been borrowed for the Christmas journey, although she was annoyed that solicitors had been involved. Quite unnecessary! They could have just asked for the money. Ridiculous people!

Ma had never really understood what I was doing in Spain in the first place, even though it was she who had sent me. Any foreign travel experience was too remote for her: languages, food, differences of one kind or another. Anyway, she was busy with her own plans. I could help her move to London. She had got rid of her last and best possessions, auctioning off the Chippendale sofa from the bay window (from where every day we had looked out over Dublin Bay), the bevelled Dresden mirror with the little white cherubs all around the edge, and the Irish-silver salver. She had always threatened to divest herself one day of all her worldly goods, which were a bother to her. That day had finally come.

Together we boarded the mail boat to cross the Irish Sea to the greater island beyond. We bore two suitcases containing small tokens of our past life as well as a wicker basket containing the remnants of her finest bone-china tea set: two cups and saucers with a violet motif, each piece wrapped carefully in pages of the Irish Times.

Ma prevailed on Paul to move in with us to a flat in South Kensington, in order to pool our meagre family resources. She wanted to "make Steph a home", she said, although she had never shown much sign of wanting to do this before.

But I could not settle down in London. I was bereft for many months – confused, lonely and miserable, overcome with a great sense of loss, like when I gave my dolls to the *niñas*. It seemed as if all the woes in my life had gathered together and conspired to haunt me. I had barely recovered from the blank space left by the death of my father and the divorce from my childhood neighbourhood that that crisis entailed. Then I was forced to end my schooldays prematurely to go to Spain – the worst aspect being the rupture from my school friends. Sometimes I believed my dire situation was due to the failure to learn the Irish language of my forefathers and mothers – or some of them anyway.

In London I missed my birthplace, as I was always to do, and the sound and feel of the sea, which I had taken for granted. The loss was more acute now that the final parting had taken place. But I had also lost Spain. It transpired that I missed Jerez almost as much as I missed Dublin.

I wrote to Javier explaining my situation and how I had been removed from Jerez abruptly, without saying goodbye to him. He responded:

Querida Estefanía:
It's not that I was surprised by your letter, but I didn't expect it, sincerely. You can be sure I have nothing against you. I consider myself your good friend and I am happy to know you. Even though we haven't seen each other for some time, I always thought about you, as I am very fond of you.

I once had a novia in Jerez. A good girl, but rich women and Jerez women have one, huge inconvenience and that's that they believe they deserve everything and they want to boss the man around from the first instant. I won't put up with this!

The problem with you, dear Estefanía, is not that you remember me, but Spain, Jerez, the sun and all things characteristic of here. It must be so different from London...

You know that my desire is to go to England. I prefer that country for the language. I tried for Germany but they didn't respond. I want to learn English and here I wouldn't have the will to learn even a single word. The minute I got a job I would go, but with the security that I was going to work and not to die of hunger.

I've always thought you and I had a lot in common. We are both unlucky because we don't know what we want. I believe I would be as free as a little bird if I could only get out of Jerez.

I understand your letter perfectly. You write an almost correct Spanish and the important thing is that I understand it very well.

It seems impossible to me that you are so far away now and I'd like you to do everything possible to find me a job there. I can't understand how people manage to go abroad and find work. Do you think at the end of one year I would speak the language? I am very cautious. I don't take risks and that also applies to speaking a language. I don't want to make a fool of myself.

Here I work with distaste. I can't find myself, because in Spain the man who aspired to be a bullfighter and didn't manage it finds emptiness and failure everywhere.

But one has to be strong and take care with people. I would like to be by your side if it's true that you find yourself very alone.

For me to go depends more on you than on me because you are the only one who can show a genuine interest in what happens to me. You can take me away from the scene of my disappointment.

Men, you say, are not interested in girls as friends, but go for the woman in them. Why do you say that? In the main, I don't think men are very romantic because they always see things in a political way unlike the way I see things. I'm not that kind of domineering man. I have always been a sensitive soul. Moreover, I always see things from a different point of view than the majority of men. I think and hope the classic Spaniard is like me – more spiritual than material and that's why I find human affections false and lacking sincerity.

If you think you can know me deeply you can trust me and tell me your intimate problems. If you find consolation in this, I can advise you. I have always opened my heart to you and I have no reserves with you.

You can count on me as the most constant of your friends…
Javier

And so Javier resumed his campaign to involve me in his existence. He had saved the story of his second and greatest disappointment until I had left the country: first were the bulls and the failure in his chosen career, second was the rich girl who had ditched him. I imagined that I was the third disappointment, as I made no attempt to rescue him. I realised immediately that I would not respond. This would be his last letter to me.

I made friends with Javier and others trapped in a feudal existence in Jerez de la Frontera after a bitter civil war. I accepted the odd world I found there as normal. I even came to believe that I shared the plight of the people I met and, for a while, I did. But their fate was not mine and I would soon shake off the fetters of my life there, and the self-absorption into which I had fallen.

In Spain I also had a brief encounter with America on a day out to the Naval Base at Rota. What I retained from that experience was a liking for smoochy music and the sweet, black tones of Nat King Cole, which always transported me back once again to the day I crossed a barrier and rode the *noria* in San Fernando: a world apart in a little green boat.